# PREDIABETES DIET COOKBOOK

Copyright © 2020 Pamela K. Daniel

All rights reserved. No part of this book may be reproduced or used in any form or by any means without written permission from the author.

# TABLE OF CONTENTS

| | |
|---|---|
| INTRODUCTION | 8 |
| AN OVERVIEW OF pre-diabetes | 10 |
| Appetizer Recipes | 24 |
| Artichoke, White Beans and Spinach Dip | 24 |
| Avocado Dip | 26 |
| Basil Pesto Stuffed Mushroom | 27 |
| Black Bean with Corn Relish | 29 |
| Zucchini and Chicken Quesadilla | 31 |
| Chickpea Polenta | 33 |
| Chipotle Savored Shrimp | 36 |
| Coconut Milk Shrimp | 38 |
| Crispy Potato with Rosemary | 40 |
| Fresh Fruit Kebabs | 42 |
| Crostini Top with Tomato Sauce | 44 |
| Fruit Salsa and Cinnamon Chips | 45 |
| Garbanzo Beans and Peanut Butter Hummus | 47 |
| Beverage RECIPES | 48 |
| Blackberry Iced Tea with Ginger and Cinnamon | 48 |

Lavender Blackberry Lemonade ................................................................ 50

Champagne with Apple Juice .................................................................... 52

Cranberry Splitzer ...................................................................................... 53

Fresh Fruits Smoothies ............................................................................... 55

Minty Green Smoothie ............................................................................... 57

Orange Zest Smoothie ................................................................................ 59

Orange Sap Smoothie ................................................................................. 61

Banana Strawberry Milkshake ................................................................... 61

Strawberry Mockarita ................................................................................. 63

Cranberry -Watermelon- Agua Fresca ....................................................... 64

BREAD RECIPES ....................................................................................... 66

Apricot and Almond Biscotti ..................................................................... 66

Apple and Corn Muffins ............................................................................ 69

Oatmeal Banana Pancake ........................................................................... 71

Buckwheat Strawberry Pancake ................................................................ 73

Chocolate Raspberry Scones ...................................................................... 75

Southwest Cornmeal Muffins .................................................................... 77

DESSERT RECIPES .................................................................................... 79

Apricot and almond crisps ......................................................................... 79

Marinated Berries in Balsamic Vinegar .................................................... 81

Chocolate Pudding Pies ................................................................ 83

Creamy Fruit Desserts ................................................................. 85

Lemon Zest Cheese ..................................................................... 87

Whole-Grain Coffeecake with Berries ........................................ 89

Rainbow Iced Pops ....................................................................... 91

Delicious Apple Pie ...................................................................... 93

Juicy Poached Pears ..................................................................... 95

MAIN DISH RECIPES .................................................................. 97

Baked Baguette with Blueberry .................................................. 97

Wild Rice with Baked Chicken ................................................... 99

French-Loaf Pizza ....................................................................... 101

Baked Macaroni with Spaghetti Sauce .................................... 103

Mealtime Burrito ........................................................................ 105

Sesame and Ginger Shrimps ..................................................... 107

Tasty Asian Pork Tenderloin ..................................................... 109

Whole-Wheat Blueberry Pancakes ........................................... 111

Smoky Frittata ............................................................................ 113

Yummy Tacos with Vegetables ................................................. 115

Thai Peanut Beef Tenderloin .................................................... 117

Vegetarian Tofu with Chili ........................................................ 119

White chicken-chili .................................................................................... 121

Grilled Asian Salmon.................................................................................123

Pasta Salad Mixed with Vegetables ................................................ 124

SA LAD RECIPES ........................................................................................ 126

Julienned Vegetables Salad ......................................................... 126

Apple Salad with Almonds and Figs .......................................... 128

Spinach and Blue Cheese Salad..................................................130

Apple and Butternut Squash Salad ...........................................132

Delicious Crab Salad .......................................................................134

Assorted Beans Salad .....................................................................136

Flavored Melon Salad .....................................................................138

Spiced Potato Salad ........................................................................ 140

SANDWICH RECIPES................................................................................ 142

Turkey and Vegetable Wrap ........................................................ 142

Tuna Salad Sandwich ...................................................................... 144

Basil and Tomato Sandwich .......................................................... 146

Coleslaw and Chicken Wrap ........................................................ 148

Chicken Burritos .............................................................................. 150

SIDES RECIPES ..........................................................................................152

Glazed Root Vegetables................................................................152

Sautéed Fresh Corn ..................................................................154

Tangy Snap Bean ....................................................................156

Creamed Swiss-chard ..............................................................158

Yummy Mashed Cauliflower ....................................................160

Minted Baby Carrots ...............................................................162

SOUP RECIPES ........................................................................164

Spicy Tomato Soup .................................................................164

Savory Fennel and Potato Soup ..............................................166

Creamy Wild Rice Soup ..........................................................167

Vichyssoise (Cold Potato and Leek Soup) ...............................170

Spiced Carrot Soup .................................................................172

Creamy Asparagus Soup .........................................................174

French Savory Onion Soup .....................................................176

Mushroom Soup with Wild Rice .............................................178

Steamed Salmon Potage .........................................................180

Petite Marmite Soup ...............................................................182

# INTRODUCTION

*Thank you for choosing the Prediabetes Diet Cookbook:* The great thing about pre-diabetes is that it's often reversible. You don't even need medications in most cases. All it may require are the right diet plan, extra healthy choices of lifestyle such as avoiding smoking and exercising, and a lot of patience and dedication.

Pre-diabetes doesn't have a single best meal or diet plan. If you ask one hundred people, "What is the pre-diabetes best diet? "You likely get a hundred different answers –and all may be right. Your plan must assist you in controlling your weight, supplying the necessary nourishing and healthy foods to reduce the risk of having diabetes and other chronic ailments, and fitting into your way of life so that it can work for you for the long term.

**The best pre-diabetes diet's goals Right Weight**

One of the most significant adjustable risk factors for pre-diabetes is extra pounds, and your chosen diet plan must help you attain and keep up a healthy weight. Whereas a "healthy" BMI is measured to be under 25kg/m2 –, which is 179 lb. for a 5 feet 11-inch man and 155 lb. for a 5 feet 6-inch woman – you may not necessarily need to get below that weight to reduce your risk. Shedding as little as five percent of your body weight or losing 8 to 10 lb, if you weigh 160 to 200 lb, will reduce the risk of diabetes.

**Right Nutrition:** Apart from weight, some nutrients are linked to enhanced health and reduce the risk of diabetes. For instance, increasing fruits, vegetables, and beans consumption, eating more whole grains rather than the refined ones, and opting for olive oil can all reduce the risk of diabetes. Avoiding sweets and refined carbohydrates such as pasta and white bread, unhealthy saturated fats from fried food, starchy vegetables, and fatty meats are examples of nutritional patterns to slow any pre-diabetes progression.

**Right Lifestyle:** If you don't choose a diabetes-friendly diet plan, it won't work. Regardless of how nutritionally perfect a diet is, it must fit into your lifestyle. Your meal plan for pre-diabetes must:

1. Include foods you love to eat

2. Rely on regular ingredients and foods that are available at your local supermarket

3. Give room for special occasions and indulgences, so you satisfy the occasional desire and fit in work event or party without feeling guilty or deviating from your diet.

4. Permit you to spend only the amount of time you want in the kitchen, instead of demanding gourmand recipes for all three meals.

# AN OVERVIEW OF PRE-DIABETES

## What is Pre-diabetes?

Pre-diabetes and diabetes are metabolic conditions. Health and behavioral problems that affect the ability of the body to metabolize and absorb or store energy that will influence the condition.

## Causes of Rise in Blood Sugar Levels

Factors that can lead to a rise in blood sugar levels include:

- Cell not responding appropriately to insulin
- Insufficient production of insulin
- Impaired insulin expression

Anyone can be affected by pre-diabetes, but some people are more susceptible to it.

Here are factors that increase the risk:

- Having low levels of activity
- Being above the age of 40 years
- Being overweight

Other factors include:

- Genetic or family traits include having a direct relation with diabetes or being from particular racial or ethnic groups.

- Having heart disease, high blood pressure or both
- Having high-density lipoprotein (LDL) or high levels of bad cholesterol and triglyceride
- Having low levels of good cholesterol, which is called high-density lipoprotein (HDL)
- Carrying extra weight around the middle, instead of the hips or having excess belly fat
- Having another particular condition, for example, gestational diabetes, polycystic ovary syndrome (PCOS), and low testosterone in men

**Warning Signs**

The pre-diabetes symptoms include:

- Increased urination and thirst
- Unexpected changes in weight
- Difficulty concentrating
- Tiredness

Acanthosis nigricans (a darkening of the skin) may also occur on various parts of the body, such as knees, knuckles, elbows, and neck. Everyday injuries can take more time to heal than normal.

People with pre-diabetes have high levels of blood sugar but still lower than the ranges of diabetes. They even have the chance to control the levels and prevent diabetes from emerging. A physician will check people's blood sugar levels with a blood glucose monitor, but individuals can do this at home as well.

According to published research in the Lancet in 2012, "five to ten percent of people with pre-diabetes worldwide develop diabetes per annum, and up to seventy percent of people with pre-diabetes go on to develop diabetes.

The study stated that taking precautionary action, such as nutritional changes can lower the risk by between 40 to 70 percent. In fact, between five to ten percent of people with pre-diabetes return to normal levels yearly.

If anyone with pre-diabetes is aware of the action to take, they have a good chance to prevent diabetes from developing.

A healthy diet and regular exercise are usually the two major lifestyle prevention plans

Changes in diet can lower the risk of pre-diabetes developing to diabetes.

The outcome of the Diabetes Prevention Program in the U.S has recommended that, in overweight people, each 1 kilogram (2.2 pounds) they lose in a year can lessen by 16 percent, their risk of developing diabetes. And after three years, the reduction in risk would have been equal to 48 percent.

A diet that will help in losing weight and managing pre-diabetes will generally include foods that are:

1. High in fiber
2. Low in calories
3. Low in fat

Such a person should consume a lot of:

- Whole grains

- Vegetables
- Protein-packed legumes
- Lean meats

They ought to be cautious to avoid added sugar. Fruits have sugar, but they provide fiber and other nutrients as well. Therefore, they may include a small amount of fruit in their diet.

## Glycemic Index

The glycemic index (GI) is a helpful apparatus for determining types of carbohydrates and for selecting the important ones. It's based on how food's sugar will penetrate the bloodstream. Those with diabetes must be mindful of how much carbohydrates and extra sugar they eat.

Nevertheless, as I have said, foods that contain sugar or carbs are not always bad. Whole grains are high in carbohydrates, and fruits have natural sugars, but they provide fiber and other nutrients. Thus, it makes them appropriate, in moderation, for people on a pre-diabetes diet.

The glycemic index is a list of foods where foods were ranked according to the rate at which they affect levels of blood sugar. The lowest score is 0, while the highest is 100. It doesn't measure the quantity of anything, but it compares how foods raise the sugar level in the blood, which 100 is the highest level.

Some foods that spike blood sugar extremely high might contain a value of more than 100. Russet potatoes score 111 on the glycemic index, according to the Oregon State University.

Here are some more sample GI values:

- Apple: 39

- Banana: 62
- Brown rice: 50
- Cornflakes: 93
- Baked beans: 40, but check the brand
- Fruit roll-ups: 99
- Full-fat milk: 41
- Muesli: 66
- Natural oatmeal: 55 on average
- Plain white baguette: 95
- Skim milk: 32
- Unsweetened apple juice: 42
- Watermelon: 72
- White rice: 89
- White spaghetti: 58
- Whole-grain bread: 51, depending on the type
- Wholemeal spaghetti: 42

The amount of carbohydrate will also be different, depending on the individual item. For instance, some apples contain more sugar than others, and manufacturers make use of varied ingredients.

The values were shown with variation in a study published in diabetes care. These values were fixed by the researcher in 2008, and they review them periodically.

**What Makes a High or Low GI Scores?**

The body digests high-fiber and whole grains foods gradually. Their sugar contents penetrate the bloodstream slowly. Foods that have fiber such as whole grains and fruit will have a lower GI, compared with foods with refined ingredients.

The body processes refined carbohydrates and sugars fast. This results in a quick rise in levels of blood sugar and high levels of glucose in the blood or a "sugar spike." Foods that have added sugar and refined carbohydrates will have a high GI score. That is the reason white bread has a higher GI score than wholemeal bread.

The people with pre-diabetes need to avoid a sugar spike. Foods that have a GI value from 55 downward tend to increase blood sugar levels gradually. Foods with GI values from 56 to 69 tend to increase blood sugar levels at a moderate pace. While those with GI values from 70 upward raise blood sugar levels quickly.

**Here are Some GI Tips:**

Whole peanut butter and whole-grain bread without additional sugar are healthful in moderation.

You cannot quickly know a food's GI value by merely looking at it.

**Here are some helpful tips**:

- Foods that have refined sugars have a higher GI value compared with those with natural sugars, like fruits.

- Whole foods contain lower GI values when compared with those processed with refined grains, for example, rice and white bread.

- Most vegetables, sweet potatoes, legumes, and whole fruit have lower GI values when compared with white starchy vegetables, such as potatoes.

- As most vegetables and fruits ripen, their sugar content rises, and their GI value goes up.

- Pastas have low GI value due to the manner their starches are bound

- Brown rice, basmati, and parboiled rice all have lower GI value when compared with jasmine rice or short grain.

- Homemade stone-cut oats or oatmeal has a lower GI value when compared with packaged oatmeal.

- Nevertheless, it's ideal to ask a dietitian or doctor for advice on what is suitable for your situation.

**Counting Carbohydrates**

Several people discover that counting carbohydrates help in ensuring the right amount of carbohydrates. Shunning carbs in totality isn't necessarily healthful. Many high carbohydrate foods, such as peas and potatoes, provide other dietary benefits. Nevertheless, a lot of low-carbohydrate diets will offer the same nutrients. A simple way of reducing carb intake is by choice of substituting low carbs for high carbs. For instance, the below starchy veggies are high in carbohydrate:

- Corn

- Peas

- Potatoes

When consuming these carbs, it's imperative to control portions to avoid blood sugar spike. A cup of corn, peas, or potatoes has approximately 30 grams of carbs. The following foods contain fewer carbohydrates per portion and are rich in fiber and other nutrients:

- Tomatoes
- Green beans
- Broccoli
- Peppers
- Asparagus
- Spinach
- Carrots
- Celery
- Zucchini
- Lettuce and other salad greens

The National Institute of Health recommends forty-five to sixty-five percent of a person's diet must consist of carbohydrates.

**Eat Regular Meals**

The people with pre-diabetes need to keep their blood sugar levels steady always. Fasting may lead to essential changes in the levels of blood sugar, but eating small meals on a regular basis could help in maintaining glucose levels.

Experts recommend:

- Eating three rightly-portioned meals often during the day, not more than six hours apart

- Making sure meals are balanced, with each having a source of carbohydrates, protein, and fat.

- A person may use the plate method to confirm if a meal is appropriately portioned.

**The Plate Method**

The Diabetes Society recommends that each meal must contain:

A healthful plate ought to be one-quarter carbohydrates, such as quinoa or brown rice, one-quarter protein food, for example, lean meat and one-half vegetables.

- One-quarter carbohydrates such as bread, rice, potatoes or pasta

- One-quarter fish, meat or an equivalent

- One-half veggies, at least two servings

- Low-fat milk, a drink of water or other healthful alternatives

- A piece of fruit

Additionally, every meal must contain at least 3 out of the 4 major food groups.

The four groups are:

- Grain foods, preferably whole grains

- Vegetables and fruit

- Fish, meat, lentils, or other options

- Milk or a substitute

For a person that desires to shed weight, research has shown that making use of a smaller plate might help to consume less.

Choose quality rather than quantity; for example, opt for fresh ingredients.

Choose sparkling water with ice and a slice of lemon, rather than alcohol or soda.

**Pre-diabetes Food to Eat**

The below table shows some of the recommended diet for pre-diabetes

| | |
|---|---|
| Non-Starchy Vegetables: low-calorie, potassium, fiber | Salad greens and fresh lettuce; celery; tomatoes; broccoli; cucumbers; mushrooms; onions; brussels sprout; snow peas; spinach; bell peppers; eggplant; zucchini; and so on; frozen vegetables (unsalted) |
| Seafood: potassium, healthy fats, protein | Salmon; crab; mackerel; shrimp; tilapia; tuna; clams; Pollock; herring |
| Legumes: potassium, protein, fiber | Beans such as pinto, garbanzo, black, and kidney beans; lentils; split and black-eyed peas; soybeans and soy products, such as edamame, |

|  |  |
|---|---|
|  | tofu, and soy milk; meat substitutes |
| Whole Grains: fiber | Wholegrain barley, pasta and cereal; oatmeal; wholegrain bread; brown rice; air-popped popcorn; farro, and quinoa |
| Starchy Vegetables: potassium, fiber | Pumpkin; corn; potatoes; sweet potatoes; green peas; winter squash |
| Plant-based fats/oils: protein (in peanuts, nuts, and seeds) fiber, healthy fats | Avocado; peanuts; olive oil; vegetable oils; natural peanut and nut butter; flaxseed; seeds; nuts |
| Low-fat dairy: calcium, protein, vitamin D, potassium | Low-fat cheese; skim milk; plain yogurt; fat-free cottage cheese |
| Fruit: potassium, fiber | Apples; berries; watermelon; cantaloupe; peaches; tangerines; pears; oranges; frozen fruit (no sugar added) |

| Hydrating beverages: low-calorie, water | Water; unsweetened tea without cream; water with mint and decaffeinated black coffee; cucumber, lemon, lime |

## Foods to Limit

- Dried fruit and fruit juice
- Starchy vegetables such as sweet potatoes, peas, corn, winter squash, and winter squash)
- Beans, lentils, and peas
- Low-fat dairy products, such as sweetened yogurt
- Grains, such as bread, cereal, oatmeal, rice, pretzels, crackers, and pasta
- Processed snack foods, for example, tortilla chips, potato chips
- Fried foods, such as fried chicken, French fries, and doughnuts
- Sweets such as cookies, ice cream, candy, cake, pastries, and pie
- Sugar-sweetened beverages such as energy drinks, sports drinks, sugar-sweetened coffee and tea, soft drinks
- Alcoholic beverages

Fruit, in moderation, is highly nutritious, containing fiber, water, vitamins, and minerals.

To lower the impact on blood sugar and keep you full for longer, enjoy fruit with a protein or healthy fat such as nut butter, a small handful of nuts seeds, or avocado.

Check with a doctor or dietitian how much of your favorite items are appropriate.

## Alcohol

Consumption of alcohol may add to the weight and the risk of diabetes as well. Many studies have found that unsafe alcohol use in men considerably increases their chances of having diabetes. Avoiding or limiting alcohol intake can help a person to reduce their weight and to control their blood sugar levels. If you're to consume alcohol, avoid sugary mixers, for example, soda.

## Other strategies

Diet only might not prevent pre-diabetes from developing into diabetes. Medication and exercise are part of other approaches.

## Exercise

A combination of dietary changes and exercise can help prevent diabetes. Physical activities can help an individual to control their blood glucose levels and reduce weight. Exercise uses up surplus blood glucose for energy and will improve insulin sensitivity.

A published article in Exercise and Sports Science Australia suggests that a person with pre-diabetes gets 125 minutes of vigorous exercise or 210 minutes of moderate exercise every week. The American Diabetes Association also recommended thirty minutes of aerobic exercises, such as brisk walking, daily or no less than five times per week. Help reducing blood sugar levels is one of the benefits of exercise.

Activities that may help include:

- Brisk walking
- Flexibility
- Running
- Strength training
- Swimming

Gardening, housework, and other activities will all contribute. It was suggested by the American Diabetes Association that people that work in a sedentary profession ought to get up and around every thirty minutes.

A doctor might prescribe metformin to assist in controlling blood glucose levels for some people with pre-diabetes. This could help, but it doesn't seem to be as effective as lifestyle measures, and metformin may have side-effects, just like all medicines. As a result of this, physicians persuade most people to make the most use of lifestyle measures.

It was found in a study published in the Annals of Internal Medicine that the doctors in America prescribed metformin for less than four percent of people living with pre-diabetes. Another study published in 2014, suggested that exercise and dietary changes are effective at curtailing the development of diabetes.

# APPETIZER RECIPES

## Artichoke, White Beans and Spinach Dip

If you desire a smoother consistency dip, you can puree the beans. Serve this dip with whole-grain crackers or raw vegetables.

**Yield: 8 Servings**

Healthy carb

Low Fat

Low Sodium

High Fiber

**Ingredients**

- 4 cups sliced raw spinach
- 1 Can (15.5 oz) artichoke hearts in water, drained
- 2 cloves garlic, crushed
- 1 tsp minced fresh thyme or ⅓ tsp dried
- 1 tsp ground black pepper
- 1 tbsp fresh crushed parsley or 1 tsp dried
- 2 tbsp shredded Parmesan cheese
- 1 cup prepared white beans, unsalted
- ½ cup r-fat sour cream

## Directions

- Preheat oven at 350°F. Combine all the ingredients in a medium mixing bowl. Pour to a ceramic dish or an oven-safe glass. After that, bake for thirty minutes. Serve Immediately.

**Nutritional fact per serving**

**Serving size**: About ½ cup

Total carbohydrate 10 g, sodium 130 mg, dietary fiber 6g, Saturated fat 1 g, monounsaturated fat Trace, trans fat 0 g, total fat 2 g, calories 78, cholesterol 6mg, protein 5 g, total sugars 1.5 g.

# Avocado Dip

Avocado is known to be a good source of lutein (an antioxidant that can protect vision) and high in monounsaturated fat.

**Yield:** 4 Servings

Low Sodium

Healthy carb

**Ingredients**

- 1 ripe avocado, peeled, pitted and crushed (approx ½ cup)
- 2 tsp sliced onion
- ½ cup fat-free sour cream
- ⅛Tsp hot sauce

**Directions**

- Combine avocado, onion, sour cream, and hot sauce in a small bowl. Mix thoroughly to blend the ingredients evenly. Dish up with sliced vegetables or baked tortilla.

Nutritional fact per serving

**Serving size**: About ¼ cup

Total carbohydrate 8 g, sodium 57 mg, dietary fiber 2.5 g, Saturated fat 1 g, monounsaturated fat 3 g, trans fat 0 g, total fat 2 g, calories 85, cholesterol 6mg, protein 5g, added sugar 0 g, total sugars trace.

# Basil Pesto Stuffed Mushroom

You can prepare this appetizer a day in advance. Place in refrigerator until ready to serve

**Yield**: 20 Servings

Low Sodium

Low Fat

**Ingredients**

20 crimini mushrooms, rinsed and stems detached

**Topping**:

- ¼ cup of melted butter
- 3 tbsp sliced fresh parsley
- 1½ cups panko breadcrumbs

**Filling**:

- 2 cups of fresh basil leaves
- 2 tbsp pumpkin seeds
- ¼ cup of fresh Parmesan cheese
- 2 tbsp lemon juice
- 1 tbsp fresh garlic
- 1 tbsp olive oil
- ½ tsp kosher salt

**Directions**

- Preheat the oven to 350 F. On a baking sheet, arrange the mushroom caps upside.

- For the topping, combine the butter, parsley, and panko in a small bowl; set aside

- For the filling, put basil, pumpkin seeds, cheese, lemon juice, garlic, oil, and salt in a food processor. Process it until well combined.

- Stuff the mushroom caps generously with the basil pesto filling. Sprinkle every mushroom with approx 1 tsp of panko topping. Lightly tap down the topping and then bake for ten to fifteen minutes or until golden brown.

**Nutritional fact per serving**

Serving size: 1 mushroom

Saturated fat 2 g, Monounsaturated fat 1 g, Trans fat 0 g, Total fat 3 g, Calories 59, Cholesterol 7 mg, Sodium 80 mg, Total carbohydrate 4 g, Total sugars 0 g, Dietary fiber 0 g, Protein 2 g.

# Black Bean with Corn Relish

If you desire a spicier relish, replace the parsley with cilantro or add chili powder to suit your taste.

**Yield**: 8 Servings

Low Sodium

Low Fat

High Fiber

Healthy carb

**Ingredients**

- 1 can (15.5 oz.) of black beans, rinsed and drained (approx 2 cups)
- 4 large tomatoes, seeded and cubed (approx 3 cups)
- 1 cup of frozen corn kernels, thawed to room temperature
- 2 garlic cloves, sliced
- ½ cup of sliced parsley
- ½ medium red onions, cubed (approx ½ cups)
- 1 yellow, red or green bell pepper, seeded and cubed (approx 1 cup)
- Juice from one lemon
- 2 tbsp of sugar

**Directions**

- Mix all the ingredients in a large bowl. Toss lightly to combine. Cover and put in the refrigerator for no less than 30 minutes to enable the flavors to blend.

**Nutritional facts per serving**

**Serving size**: Approx 1 cup

Calories 112, Cholesterol 0 mg, Dietary fiber 6 g, Sodium 93 mg, Trans fat 0 g, Saturated fat Trace, Monounsaturated fat Trace, Total fat 0.5 g, Protein 5 g, Total carbohydrate 22 g, Total sugars 3 g.

# Zucchini and Chicken Quesadilla

**Yield:** 8 Servings

High Fiber

Healthy carb

**Ingredients**

- 8 oz. of cubed cooked chicken breast
- 1 large tomato, diced
- 1 cup of cubed zucchini
- ½ cup of diced red onion
- 1 jalapeno pepper, diced
- 1 yellow bell pepper, diced
- 1 tbsp of diced garlic
- 1 cup of shredded cheddar cheese
- 2 whole-wheat tortillas, 12-inch long
- 1 tsp of Tabasco sauce
- ½ tsp of cumin
- 1 lime

**Directions**

- Preheat the oven to 375° F temperature. Combine the chicken, tomato, zucchini, onion, bell pepper, garlic, and jalapeno in a medium bowl. Slash the lime and squeeze the juice on top of the chicken combination. Add the cumin, Tabasco, and cheese, then mix well.

- Place a large nonstick sauté pan over medium heat. Lay one of the tortillas flat in the pan and spread half of the chicken mixture on one side. Cover the mixture by folding the tortilla. Heat each side of the tortilla to lightly brown.

- Take the second tortilla and repeat the process. On a baking sheet, put tortillas and bake in the preheated oven for ten to fifteen minutes or until the ingredients are warm and the cheese is melted all through. Serve warm.

## Nutritional facts per serving

**Serving size**: ½ quesadilla

Saturated fat 8 g, Monounsaturated fat 3 g, Trans fat 0 g, Total fat 14 g, Calories 345, Sodium 649 mg, Cholesterol 71 mg, Dietary fiber 16 g, Total sugars 3 g, Protein 27 g, Total carbohydrate 28 g.

# Chickpea Polenta

You can find chickpea flour in Indian or Italian markets.

**Yield**: 8 Servings

Healthy carb

**Ingredients**

**For the polenta**:

- 1¾ cups of chickpea flour
- 1 cup of chicken broth
- 2 cups of plain soy milk
- 3 cloves garlic, sliced
- ½ tbsp of extra-virgin olive oil
- 1 tbsp chopped fresh basil, oregano or thyme, or 1 tsp of dried one
- ¼ tsp of black pepper, freshly ground
- 1 tsp of dry mustard
- 3 egg whites

**For the topping**:

- ½ tbsp extra-virgin olive oil
- ½ yellow onion, crushed
- ¼ cup roughly chopped pitted Kalamata olives
- 2 tbsp shredded Parmesan cheese

- ¼ cup of sun-dried tomatoes, soaked in water to rehydrate, drained and sliced
- 2 tbsp thinly cut fresh flat-leaf (Italian) parsley

**Directions**

- Combine the flour, broth, soy milk olive oil, thyme, pepper, and mustard in a food processor or blender. Process the ingredients until well blended. Pour the mixture into a large bowl and refrigerate for one hour.
- Preheat the oven to 425° F temperature. Prepare a nine by 13" baking pan and lightly coat it with cooking spray
- Beat the egg whites in a large, clean mixing bowl until stiff peaks form.
- Add the mixture into the prepared pan. Bake the dough in the preheated oven for about 15 minutes or until puffed and lightly browned around the edges. Leave it for 15 minutes to cool.
- Heat the broiler. Place the rack 4 inches from the source of heat.
- Prepare the toppings while the polenta is cooling. Place a small sauté pan over medium-high heat and pour the olive oil. Add onion; cook for about 5 minutes or until lightly golden and soft. Add the tomatoes and olives and cook for one minute. Remove the heat source.
- Cautiously ladle the onion mixture evenly over the baked polenta and sprinkle with the cheese. Broil it for about one minute until the top is lightly browned. And then sprinkle with the parsley.

- Transfer it to wire rack and leave for ten minutes to cool. Slice into eight squares and then slice the squares on the slanting into sixteen wedges. Serve immediately.

**Nutritional facts per serving**

**Serving size**: 2 wedges

Saturated fat 1 g, Trans fat 0 g, Monounsaturated fat 2 g, Total fat 5 g, Sodium 160 mg, Calories 157, Dietary fiber 3 g, Total carbohydrate 20 g, Cholesterol 2 mg, Protein 8 g, Added sugars 0 g, Total sugars 4 g.

# Chipotle Savored Shrimp

Shrimp is cooked when the flesh turns opaque and white.

**Yield**: 4 Servings

Low Sodium

Low Fat

**Ingredients**

- 1 pound of fresh shrimp, peeled and deveined
- 2 tbsp of tomato paste
- ½ tsp of extra-virgin olive oil
- ½ tsp of chipotle chili powder
- ½ tsp crushed garlic
- ½ tsp of sliced fresh oregano
- 1½ tsp of water

**Directions**

- In cold water, wash and rinse shrimp. Use a paper towel to pat dry it. Put in a plate and set aside.
- For marinade, whisk together the oil, water, and tomato paste in a small bowl. Add oregano, chili powder, and garlic. Mix well to combine.
- Spread the marinade on the two sides of the shrimp with a brush and refrigerate.

- Heat a broiler or gas grill; afar from the source of heat, lightly coat the broiler pan or grill rack with cooking spray. Situate the cooking rack four to six inches from the source of heat.

- Place the shrimp on skewers or grill basket and put on the grill. After three to four minutes, turn the shrimp. The cooking time depends on the intensity of the heat from the fire, so watch cautiously

- Return to a plate and serve when hot.

**Nutritional facts per serving**

**Serving size**: ¼ of the recipe

Calories 109, Cholesterol 182 mg, Total carbohydrate 2 g, Monounsaturated fat 0.5 g, Saturated fat Trace, Trans fat Trace, Total fat 1 g, Sodium 139 mg, Added sugars 0 g, Total sugars 0 g, Dietary fiber 0.5 g, Protein 23 g.

# Coconut Milk Shrimp

Smaller shrimp can be used, just plan for less baking time and less breading.

**Yield**: 4 Servings

**Ingredients**

- 12 large shrimp, peeled and deveined
- ½ cup of coconut milk
- ¼ cup of panko breadcrumbs
- ¼ cup of sweetened coconut
- ½ tsp of kosher salt

**Directions**

- Preheat the oven to 375° F temperature. Coat a baking sheet lightly, using cooking spray.
- Put the panko, coconut, and salt in a food processor. Process it until the mixture is well blended and then transfer to a small bowl. In a separate small bowl, add the coconut milk.
- Dip each shrimp in the coconut milk and also in the panko mixture. Put the shrimp on the baking sheet and lightly coat the top with cooking spray. Bake in the \preheated oven for 10 to 15 minute until it turns golden brown

**Nutritional fact per serving**

**Serving size**: 2 shrimp

Dietary fiber 0 g, Calories 75 Trans fat 0 g, Saturated fat 2 g, Monounsaturated fat 2 g, Total fat 4 g, Sodium 396 mg, Cholesterol 48 mg, Total sugars 2 g, Total carbohydrate 4 g, Protein 5 g

# Crispy Potato with Rosemary

Any spices or herbs can be used to season the potato skins. Try cayenne pepper, fresh basil, thyme, garlic, tarragon, chives, dill or caraway seed.

**Yield**: 2 Servings

Healthy carb

Low Sodium

Low Fat

High Fiber

**Ingredients**

- 2 medium russet potatoes
- ⅛Tsp of freshly ground black pepper
- 1 tbsp crushed fresh rosemary
- Butter-flavor cooking spray

**Directions**

- Preheat the oven to 375 F temperatures.
- Wash, rinse the potatoes and pierce with a fork. Put in the preheated oven for about one hour or until the skins are crunchy.
- Cautiously cut the hot potatoes in half and ladle out the pulp, leaving approx ⅛inch of the potato pulp attached to the skin. Keep them fresh for another use.

- Sprinkle the inner of each potato skin with cooking spray. Add the pepper and rosemary. Put the skin back into the oven for five to ten minutes. Serve warm.

**Nutritional facts per serving**

**Serving size**: 2 pieces

Calories 50, Cholesterol 0 mg, Total carbohydrate 10 g, Dietary fiber 4 g, Saturated fat Trace, Monounsaturated fat Trace, Trans fat 0 g, Sodium 12 mg, Total fat Trace, Added sugars 0 g, Total sugars 1 g, Protein 2 g.

# Fresh Fruit Kebabs

Any type of fruit can be used to prepare these kebabs, including more exotic varieties such as prickly pears, kumquats, or star fruit. Dip in orange or pineapple juice to prevent fruit from browning.

**Yield**: 2 Servings

Low Sodium

Low Fat

**Ingredients**

- 1 tsp of lime zest
- 6 oz of sugar-free, low-fat lemon yogurt
- 1 tsp of fresh lime juice
- 4 pineapple chunks (approx ½ inch each)
- 4 strawberries
- 4 red grapes
- 1 kiwi, peeled and quartered
- ½ bananas cut into 4 ½-inch chunks
- 4 wooden skewers

**Directions**

- Whisk together the lime zest, yogurt, and lime juice in a small mixing bowl. Cover and place in the refrigerator until needed.

- Thread one of each fruit onto the skewer. Do the same with the other skewers until the fruit is gone. Serve with the yogurt lime dip.

**Nutritional facts per serving**

**Serving size**: 2 fruit kebabs

Cholesterol 5 mg, Calories 190, Dietary fiber 4 g, Trans fat 0 g, Monounsaturated fat Trace, Saturated fat 1 g, Total fat 2 g, Total carbohydrate 39 mg, Protein 4 g, Sodium 53 mg, Added sugars 6 g.

# Crostini Top with Tomato Sauce

Crostini means little toasts in Italy. You will top these little toasts with tomato, garlic, and basil mixture.

**Yield**: 4 Servings

**Ingredients**

- ¼ pound of crispy Italian peasant bread, cut into 4 slices and toasted
- 4 plum tomatoes, sliced
- 1 clove garlic, crushed
- ¼ cup of crushed fresh basil
- 2 tsp of olive oil
- Freshly ground pepper

**Directions**

- In a medium mixing bowl, combine tomatoes, garlic, basil, and oil. Cover and leave it for 30 minutes. To serve, spread the tomato mixture over the toast. Serve at room temperature.

**Nutritional facts per serving**

**Serving size**: 1 slice

Sodium 176 mg, Dietary fiber 1 g, Calories 107, Trans fat 0 g, Saturated fat 0.6 g, Total fat 3.5 g, Total carbohydrate 16 g, Cholesterol 0 mg, Added sugars 0 g, Protein 3 g.

# Fruit Salsa and Cinnamon Chips

**Yield:** 8 servings

Low Fat

Healthy carb

High Fiber

**Ingredients**

**For tortilla chips:**

- 8 fat-free whole-wheat tortillas
- ½ tbsp of cinnamon
- 1 tbsp of sugar
- Cooking spray

**For the fruit salsa:**

- 3 cups of cubed fresh fruit, such as strawberries, oranges, grapes, apples, kiwi, or other fresh fruit
- 2 tbsp of orange juice
- 1 tbsp of honey
- 2 tbsp of no-sugar jam of any flavor

**Directions**

- Preheat the oven to 350° F temperature. Cut each of the tortillas into 8 wedges. Place pieces on two baking sheets. Ensure they are not overlapping. Spray the tortilla pieces with cooking spray.

- Combine cinnamon and sugar in a small bowl. Sprinkle the sugar mixture evenly over the tortilla wedges. Bake the tortillas until the pieces are crispy for about 10 minutes.

- Cut the fruit into cubes and combine them in a large bowl. Whisk together orange juice, honey, and jam in a separate bowl. After that, pour the mixture over the cubed fruit and mix softly. Use a plastic wrap to cover the bowl and then put it in the refrigerator for about 3 hours.

- Serve as a topping or dip for the sweet tortilla chips.

**Nutritional facts per serving**

**Serving size**: About eight chips and ⅓ cup of salsa

Calories 105, Total carbohydrate 24 g, Dietary fiber 10 g, Sodium 181 mg, Saturated fat Trace, Trans fat Trace, Monounsaturated fat Trace, Total fat Trace, Added sugars 4 g, Total sugars 8 g, Protein 2 g, Cholesterol 0 mg.

# Garbanzo Beans and Peanut Butter Hummus

You can serve this traditional hummus as a dip for celery and apple or spread on sandwiches.

**Yield**: 16 Servings

**Ingredients**

- 1 cup of water
- 2 cups of garbanzo beans
- ¼ cup of natural peanut butter
- ½ cup of powdered peanut butter
- 1 tsp of vanilla extract
- 2 tbsp of brown sugar

**Directions**

- In a food processor, add all the ingredients and process it until well blended. You can refrigerate this for up to 7 days.

**Nutritional facts per serving**

**Serving size**: 2 tbsp

Dietary fiber 4 g, Calories 135, Saturated fat 0 g, Trans fat 0 g, Monounsaturated fat 1 g, Total fat 4 g, Total carbohydrate 19 g, Sodium 47 mg Cholesterol 0 mg, Total sugars 4 g, Protein 7 g.

# BEVERAGE RECIPES

# Blackberry Iced Tea with Ginger and Cinnamon

**Yield**: 6 Servings

Low Sodium

Low Fat

**Ingredients**

- 6 cups of water
- 12 bags of blackberry herbal tea
- 1 cup of unsweetened cranberry juice
- 8 3-inch-long cinnamon sticks
- Sweetener, to taste
- 1 tbsp of crushed fresh ginger
- Crushed Ice cubes

**Directions**

- Heat water in a large saucepot to just before boiling: add the tea bags, ginger, and two of the cinnamon sticks. Take it out of heat, cover, and allow it to steep for about fifteen minutes.

- Sieve the mixture in a fine-mesh sieve, put over a pitcher. Add the sweetener and juice to taste. Place in the refrigerator until very chilly.

- To dish up, fill six glasses with the crushed ice cubes. Pour the tea on top of the ice and garnish with the remaining cinnamon sticks. Dish up immediately.

**Nutritional facts per serving**

**Serving size**: 1 cup

Calories 25, Total carbohydrate 6 g, Cholesterol 0 mg, Dietary fiber Trace, Trans fat 0 g, Saturated fat 0 g, Monounsaturated fat 0 g, Total fat 0 g, Sodium 3 mg, Added sugars 0 g, Total sugars 5 g, Protein Trace.

# Lavender Blackberry Lemonade

For best results, squeeze about ten large lemons or opt for fresh lemon juice and measure lavender carefully.

**Yield**: 16 Servings

Healthy carb

Low Fat

Low Sodium

**Ingredients**

- 2 cups of water
- 1 package of blueberries (16 ounces)
- 1 tbsp of dried lavender flowers
- ¼ cup of granulated sugar
- 2 tbsp of Splenda sweetener
- 1 cup of lemon juice
- Coldwater

**Directions**

- Add 4 cups of ice in a 1-gallon pitcher and set aside. Bring 2 the cups of water to a boil over medium heat in a medium pan. Add the blueberries, lavender, and sugar to the saucepan. Leave to boil for 5 minutes or until the sugar has dissolved, and blueberries have popped.
- Sieve the blueberry mixture over the pitcher containing ice. After that, dispose of the remaining blueberry mix.

Add the Splenda and lemon juice to the pitcher. Fill with cold water and mix thoroughly.

**Nutritional facts per serving**

**Serving size**: 8 oz

Cholesterol 0 mg, Sodium 7 mg, Cholesterol 0 mg, Saturated fat 0 g, Calories 33, Monounsaturated fat 0 g, Trans fat 0 g, Total fat 0 g, Total carbohydrate 8 g, Total sugars 7 g, Dietary fiber 0 g, Protein 0 g.

# Champagne with Apple Juice

This champagne substitute has all the sparkle and taste but half the calories of the real thing.

**Yield**: 4 Servings

Low Fat

Low Sodium

**Ingredients**

- 2 cups of unsweetened apple cider or apple juice
- 2 cups of sparkling water, lemon-flavored
- 1½ tsp of fresh lemon juice

**Directions**

- Chill a wine glass or champagne. Combine the sparkling water, apple juice, and lemon juice in a glass. Serve chill.

**Nutritional facts per serving**

**Serving size**: About ⅔ cup (5 oz)

Calories 55, Cholesterol 0 mg, Sodium 4 mg, saturated fat 0 g, Monounsaturated fat 0 g, Trans fat 0 g,

Total fat 0 g, Total carbohydrate 14 g, Trans fat 0 g, Dietary fiber 0 g, Added sugars 0 g, Protein Trace.

# Cranberry Splitzer

**Yield:** 10 Servings

Low Sodium

Low Fat

**Ingredients**

- 10 lemon or lime wedges
- 1 quart of low-calorie cranberry juice
- 1 quart of carbonated water
- ½ cup of fresh lemon juice
- 1 cup of raspberry sherbet
- ¼ cup of sugar

**Directions**

- Refrigerate the carbonated water, lemon juice, and cranberry juice until cold.
- Combine the lemon juice, cranberry juice, carbonated water, sherbet, and sugar in a large pitcher. In tall, chilled glasses, pour the lemon mixture and garnish with lime or lemon wedges. Dish up immediately.

**Nutritional facts per serving**

**Serving size:** 1 cup

Total carbohydrate 24 g, Cholesterol 0 mg, Dietary fiber Trace, Total fat Trace, Calories 100, Saturated fat Trace,

Monounsaturated fat Trace, Trans fat 0 g, Sodium 9 mg, Added sugars 10 g, Total sugars 22 g, Protein Trace.

# Fresh Fruits Smoothies

Ingredients can be prepared ahead of time and be refrigerated until they are ready to be blended.

**Yield:** 8 Servings

Healthy carb

Low Fat

Low Sodium

**Ingredients**

- 1 cup of fresh strawberries
- 1 cup of fresh pineapple chunks
- 1 cup of cold water
- ½ cup of cantaloupe or any other melon chunks
- Juice of 2 oranges
- 1 tbsp of honey

**Directions**

- Remove the strawberries stems. Remove rind from the melon and pineapple. Cut them into pieces. In a blender, add all the ingredients and puree until well blended. Serve when chill.

**Nutritional facts per serving**

**Serving size**: 8 oz

Calories 72, Total carbohydrate 17 g, Cholesterol 0 mg, Trans fat 0 g, Saturated fat 0 g, Monounsaturated fat 0 g, Total fat 0 g, Dietary fiber 1 g, Added sugars 4 g, Sodium 7 mg, Total sugars 13 g, Protein 1 g.

# Minty Green Smoothie

**Yield**: Servings

Low Sodium

Healthy carb

Low Fat

**Ingredients**

- Juice of 1 lemon (about 4 tbsp)
- 1 banana
- 2 oz of fresh raw baby spinach (approx 2 cups)
- ½ cup of strawberries
- ½ cup of other berries, such as blueberries or blackberries
- 1 cup of ice or cold water
- Fresh mint to taste

**Directions**

- In a blender, add all the ingredients and puree until smooth. Enjoy.

**Nutritional fact per serving**

**Serving size**: 6 fluid oz

Calories 64, Sodium 15 mg, Total carbohydrate 12 g, Saturated fat Trace, Dietary fiber 2 g, Monounsaturated fat Trace, Trans fat 0 g, Total fat Trace, Cholesterol 0 mg, Added sugars 0 g, Protein 1 g, Total sugars 7 g

# Orange Zest Smoothie

For best results, make use of freshly squeezed orange juice and ice-cold soy milk.

**Yield**: 4 Servings

Low Sodium

Low Fat

**Ingredients**

- 1 ½ cup of chilled orange juice
- ⅓ Cup of soft or silken tofu
- 1 cup of chilled light vanilla soy milk
- 1 tsp of grated orange zest
- 1 tbsp of dark honey
- 4 peeled orange segments (approx. half an orange)
- 5 ice cubes
- ⅓ Tsp of vanilla extract

**Directions**

- Combine the soy milk, orange juice, vanilla, orange zest, honey, tofu, and ice cubes in a blender. Puree for about 30 seconds, until frothy and smooth.
- Prepare tall, chilled glasses and pour the mixture into them. Garnish each of the glasses with an orange segment.

**Nutritional facts per serving**

**Serving size**: 1 cup (8 fluid ounces)

Calories 101, Total carbohydrate 20 g, Sodium 40 mg, Dietary fiber 1 g, Saturated fat < 1 g, Trans fat 0 g, Monounsaturated fat < 1 g, Total fat 1 g, Cholesterol 0 mg, Total sugars 14 g, Protein 3 g, Added sugars 4 g.

# Orange Sap Smoothie

Orange juice is an excellent source of potassium, a mineral that helps control cell function and blood pressure.

**Yield**: 2 Servings

Low Sodium

Low Fat

**Ingredients**

- ¼ cup of frozen no-sugar orange juice concentrate
- ¾ cup of fat-free milk
- 1 cup of no-sugar, fat-free vanilla frozen yogurt

**Directions**

- Combine the orange juice, frozen yogurt, and milk in a blender. Puree until well blended. Pour the smoothie into tall, chilled glasses and dish up immediately.

**Nutritional facts per serving**

**Serving size**: 1 cup

Calories 200, Cholesterol 4 mg, Dietary fiber 5 g, Sodium 177 mg, Monounsaturated fat Trace, Trans fat 0 g, Saturated fat Trace, Total fat Trace, Total carbohydrate 41 g, Protein 12 g, Added sugars 0 g, Total sugars 26 g.

# Banana Strawberry Milkshake

For this recipe, 1 cup of chopped fresh peaches can be used to replace strawberries for an equally juicy treat.

**Yield**: 2 Servings

Low Fat

Low Sodium

High Fiber

**Ingredients**

- 6 frozen strawberries, sliced
- ½ cup of soy milk
- 1 medium banana
- 2 fresh strawberries, chopped
- 1 cup of fat-free vanilla frozen yogurt

**Directions**

- Combine the banana, frozen yogurt, frozen strawberries, and soy milk in a blender. Puree until well blended.
- In tall, chilled glasses, pour the mixture and garnish each glass with fresh strawberries chopped. Serve immediately.
- Pour into tall, frosty glasses and garnish each with fresh strawberry slices. Serve immediately.

**Nutritional facts per serving**

**Serving size**: 1 cup

Calories 183, Total carbohydrate 40 g, Saturated fat trace, Monounsaturated fat 0 g, Dietary fiber 8 g, Sodium 117 mg, Cholesterol 0 mg, Trans fat 0 g, Total fat 1 g, Added sugars 17 g, Protein 6 g.

# Strawberry Mockarita

**Yield**: 6 Servings

Low Fat

Low Sodium

Healthy carb

**Ingredients**

- ¼ cup of lime juice
- 4 cups of chopped strawberries
- ¼ cup of sugar
- 2 cups of ice
- 2 cups of water

**Directions**

- Puree all the ingredients in a blender until well blended. Serve immediately or refrigerate.

**Nutritional facts per serving**

**Serving size**: 8 ounces

Dietary fiber 2 g, Calories 64, Sodium 3 mg, Monounsaturated fat 0 g, Trans fat 0 g, Saturated fat 0 g, Total fat 0 g, Total carbohydrate 16 g, Cholesterol 0 mg, Protein 1 g, Total sugars 13 g.

# Cranberry -Watermelon- Agua Fresca

Agua frescas res fresh-fruit drinks popularly known in Mexico.

**Yield**: 6 Servings

Low Fat

Low Sodium

**Ingredients**

- 2 ½ pounds of peeled, seeded and cubed watermelon (about 7 cups)
- ¼ cup of fresh lime juice
- 1 cup of fruit-sweetened cranberry juice
- 1 lime, slice into 6

**Directions**

- Put the watermelon in a food processor or blender and process until smooth. Take the processed melon through a mesh sieve placed over a container to separate the pulp from the juice.
- In a large pitcher, pour the juice and add the lime and cranberry juice. Stir until well combined.
- Place juice inside the refrigerator to turn cold. In chilled glasses, pour the juice and garnish each of the glasses with a slice of lime.
- Refrigerate until very cold. Pour into tall chilled glasses and garnish each with a slice of lime.

**Nutritional facts per serving**

**Serving size**: About ¾ cup

Calories 84, Total carbohydrate 20 g, Sodium 9 mg, Trans fat 0 g, Saturated fat 0 g, Cholesterol 0 mg, Monounsaturated fat 0 g, Dietary fiber 1 g, Total fat 0 g, Added sugars 0 g, Protein 1 g, Total sugars 16 g.

# BREAD RECIPES

## Apricot and Almond Biscotti

This yummy cookie goes well with coffee or tea.

Yield: 24 Servings

Healthy carb

Low Fat

Low Sodium

**Ingredient**

- ¾ cup of all-purpose (plain) flour
- ¾ cup of whole-wheat flour
- 1 tsp of baking powder
- ¼ cup of tightly packed brown sugar
- ¼ cup of coarsely chopped almonds
- ⅔ cup of sliced dried apricots
- 2 tbsp of 1% low-fat milk
- 2 eggs, lightly beaten
- 2 tbsp of canola oil
- 2 tbsp of dark honey
- ½ tsp of almond extract

## Directions

- Preheat the oven to 350° F temperature.

- Combine the flour, baking powder, and brown sugar in a large container and whisk to blend. Add the almond extract, honey, canola oil, milk, and eggs. Use a wooden spoon to stir until the dough starts coming together. Then, add the almonds and apricots. With flour in your hands, mix them until the mixture is well combined.

- On a long plastic sheet, place the dough, wrap and shape it with your hand into a flattened log 3 inches wide, 12 inches long, and about an inch high. Raise the plastic sheet to transfer the dough into a non-stick baking sheet.

- Place the dough inside preheated oven and bake for 25 to 30 minutes, until lightly browned. Afterward, move the dough to another baking sheet to cool for ten minutes. Let the oven remain at 350° F.

- Once cooled. Place the dough on a cutting board. Cut diagonally into 24 slices ½ inch wide using a serrated knife. On the baking sheet, position the slices, cut-side down, and then return to the oven.

- Bake for another 15 to 20 minutes, until crisp. Remove from oven and place on a wire rack to cool completely. Serve the cookies immediately or store in an airtight container.

## Nutritional facts per serving

**Serving size**: 1 cookie

Total carbohydrate 12 g, Cholesterol 15 mg, Calories 75, Monounsaturated fat 1 g, Trans fat Trace, Saturated fat Trace,

Total fat 2 g, Sodium 17 mg, Added sugars 2 g, Total sugars 6 g, Dietary fiber 1 g, Protein 2 g

# Apple and Corn Muffins

Granny Smith, Gala, Cortland, and Braeburn are good baking apples.

**Yield**: 12 muffins

Low Fat

Low Sodium

**Ingredients**

- 1 apple, cored, peeled and coarsely chopped
- 2 cups of all-purpose (plain) flour
- ½ cup of yellow cornmeal
- ½ cup of corn kernels (frozen or fresh)
- ¼ cup of packed brown sugar
- ¾ cup of fat-free milk
- 1 tbsp of baking powder
- 2 egg whites
- ¼ tsp of salt

**Directions**

- Preheat the oven to 425° F temperature. Line a 12-cup muffin pan with foil liners or paper.
- Combine flour, baking powder, salt, and sugar in a large container. With a wooden spoon, stir the mixture to combine well.

- Combine egg whites and milk in another bowl. Add corn kernels and chopped apple. Whisk to blend evenly and add to the flour mixture. Mix softly until the dry ingredients are a bit humid. The batter should be lumpy.
- Fill each of the muffin cups ⅔ full and bake for about thirty minutes. When they are done, tops of muffins will spring back to the touch.

**Nutritional facts per serving**

**Serving size**: 1 muffin

Dietary fiber 1 g, Total carbohydrate 26 g, Cholesterol Trace, Calories 120, Trans fat 0 g, Saturated fat Trace, Monounsaturated fat Trace, Sodium 128 mg, Total fat < 1 g, Added sugars 4 g, Protein 4 g, Total sugars 7 g

# Oatmeal Banana Pancake

Substitute ¼ cup of whole-wheat flour with ground pumpkin seeds or ground flaxseeds to achieve a nuttier flavor.

**Yield:** 4 Servings

Healthy carb

Low Fat

**Ingredients**

- ½ cup of conventional rolled oats
- 2 tbsp of brown sugar
- 2 tbsp of canola oil
- ½ cup of all-purpose (plain) flour
- ½ cup of whole-wheat flour
- ¼ tsp of baking soda
- 1 cup of boiling water or hot water
- 1½ tsp of baking powder
- ¼ tsp of ground cinnamon
- ¼ cup of fat-free plain yogurt
- 1 egg
- ½ cup of skim milk
- 1 crushed banana
- ¼ tsp of salt

## Directions

- Add the oat and boiling water in a large bowl. Leave it for one to two minutes until oats are tender and creamy. Stir in sugar and oil: then, set it aside to cool a bit.

- Combine the flours, ground cinnamon, baking soda, salt, and baking powder in a medium container. Whisk the mixture to combine well.

- After that, add the banana, yogurt, and milk to the oats. Stir to combine well and whisk in the egg. Pour the flour mixture over the oat mixture and stir thoroughly to moisten. Prepare medium heat and place a nonstick saucepan over it.

- Once the pan is hot, spoon ¼ cup of pancake batter into it. Heat the pancake until its edges are lightly browned, and the top surface is covered with bubbles, for about 2 minutes. Turn the pancake and heat for another 2 minutes. Do the same to the remaining batter. Enjoy.

**Nutritional facts per serving**

**Serving size:** 3 pancakes

Cholesterol 48 mg, Calories 288, Dietary fiber 3 g, Monounsaturated fat 6 g, Trans fat 0 g, Saturated fat 0 g, Total fat 9 g, Sodium 453 mg, Total carbohydrate 45 g, Total sugars 12 g, Protein 9 g.

# Buckwheat Strawberry Pancake

Instead of maple syrup, top these pancakes with sliced strawberries or other types of fresh fruit such as sliced bananas or peaches.

**Yield:** 6 Servings

Healthy carb

Low Fat

**Ingredients**

- ½ cup of all-purpose (plain) flour
- ½ cup of fat-free milk
- 1 tbsp of canola oil
- 2 egg whites
- 1 tbsp of baking powder
- ½ cup of buckwheat flour
- 3 cups of sliced fresh strawberries
- 1 tbsp of sugar
- ½ cup of sparkling water

**Directions**

- Whisk together the milk, egg white, and canola oil in a small bowl.

- In a large container, mix the flour, sugar and baking powder. Then add the egg white mixture, follow by the sparkling water. Stir thoroughly until a bit moistened.

- Prepare medium heat and place a non-stick saucepan over it. Once the pan is hot, spoon ½ cup of pancake batter into it. Heat the pancake until its edges are lightly browned, and the top surface is covered with bubbles, for about 2 minutes. Turn the pancake and heat for another two to three minutes, until the pancake is done. Do the same to the remaining batter.

- To serve, top each of the pancake plates with ½ cup of sliced strawberries.

**Nutritional fact per serving**

**Serving size**: 2 small pancakes

Total carbohydrate 24 g, Calories 143, Dietary fiber 3 g, Sodium 150 mg, Cholesterol Trace, Monounsaturated fat 2 g, Trans fat 0 g, Saturated fat Trace, Total fat 3 g, Protein 5 g, Added sugars 2 g, Total sugars 6.5 g

# Chocolate Raspberry Scones

In the United Kingdom, a scone is popularly quick bread that serves as a teatime treat.

**Yield:** 12 Servings

Healthy carb

**Ingredients**

- 1 cup of all-purpose (plain) flour
- 1 cup of whole-wheat pastry flour
- ¼ tsp of baking soda
- 1 tbsp of baking powder
- 1 cup and 2 tbsp of plain fat-free yogurt
- ½ cup of frozen or fresh raspberries
- ⅓ Cup of Trans fat-free buttery spread
- 2 tbsp of honey
- ¼ cup of miniature chocolate chips
- 1 cup and 2 tbsp of plain fat-free yogurt
- ¼ tsp of cinnamon
- ½ tsp of sugar

**Directions**

- Preheat the oven to 400°F temperature.

- In a large bowl, combine flours, baking soda, and baking powder. Add in the buttery spread and mix until crumbly. Stir in chocolate chips and berries.

- In a small bowl, mix honey and yogurt. Pour the yogurt mixture over the flour mixture. Stir until well combined.

- Put the dough on a countertop. Knead 1 or 2 times. Shape into a ½ inch thick round and cut into 12 wedges. Lightly grease s baking sheet and place the dough.

- In a small bowl, combine the cinnamon and sugar and sprinkle on top of scones. Place it in the preheated oven and bake for 10 to 12 minutes.

**Nutritional facts per serving**

**Serving size**: 1 scone

Total carbohydrate 22 g, Calories 149, Sodium 143 mg, Monounsaturated fat 2 g, Trans fat Trace, Saturated fat 1.5 g, Saturated fat 1.5 g, Total fat 5 g, Cholesterol Trace, Dietary fiber 2 Protein 4 g

# Southwest Cornmeal Muffins

Stone-ground cornmeal is a good source of nutrients such as potassium, vitamin C, and fiber.

**Yields:** 12 muffins

Low Fat

**Ingredients**

- 2 tsp of baking powder
- 1 cup of all-purpose flour
- 1 cup of fat-free milk
- 1¼ cups of stone-ground cornmeal
- 4 tbsp of vegetable oil
- ½ cup of egg substitute
- ½ green bell pepper, sliced
- 1 cup of cream-style or fresh corn
- ¼ cup of sugar

**Directions**

- Preheat the oven to a temperature of 400° F. and line a 12-Cup muffin pan with foil liners or paper.
- After that, in a medium container, add the flour, baking powder, and sugar. Stir to combine well.
- In another container, combine the cornmeal, milk, green pepper, corn, oil, and egg substitute. Pour over the flour

mixture and stir until turn moistened, but the batter is still a bit lumpy.

- Fill each of the muffin cups ⅔ full and bake for about thirty minutes. When they are done, tops of muffins will spring back to the touch. Enjoy.

**Nutritional facts per serving**

**Serving size**: 1 muffin

Total carbohydrate 26 g, Sodium 138 mg, Saturated fat 1 g, Monounsaturated fat 2 g, Trans fat 0 g, Added sugars 7 g, Total fat 5 g, Cholesterol trace, Protein 4 g, Dietary fiber 1.5 g, Calories 167.

# DESSERT RECIPES

## Apricot and almond crisps

You can use certified gluten-free oats to make this apricot dessert gluten-free

**Yield:** 6 Servings

Low Sodium

**Ingredients**

- 1 pound of apricots, cut into two, remove the pits and chop
- ½ cup of almonds, sliced
- 1 tbsp of oats (certified gluten-free
- 1 tsp of olive oil
- 1 tsp of anise seeds
- 2 tsp of honey

**Directions**

- Preheat oven to 350° F temperature.
- Brush the olive oil inside a 9-inch glass pie dish. Place the chopped apricot inside the pie dish. Drizzle with oats, almonds, and anise seeds over the apricot. And then, sprinkle with honey.

- Place in the preheated oven and bake until apricots are bubbling up, and almond topping is golden brown, about 25 minutes. Serve warm

**Nutritional facts per serving**

**Serving size:** About ½ cup

Dietary fiber 3 g, Total carbohydrate 17 g, Calories 134, Monounsaturated fat 4, Trans fat Trace, Saturated fat 0.5 g, Total fat 6 g, Cholesterol 0 mg, Added sugars 6 g, Protein 3 g, Sodium 1 mg.

# Marinated Berries in Balsamic Vinegar

Garnish this recipe with a sprig of fresh mint. Use blackberries, gooseberries, and huckleberries for a different taste.

**Yield:** 2 Servings

Low Sodium

**Ingredients**

- ½ cup of chopped raspberries
- ½ cup of chopped blueberries
- ½ cup of chopped strawberries
- ¼ cup of balsamic vinegar
- 2 shortbread biscuits
- 1 tsp of vanilla extract
- 2 tbsp of brown sugar

**Directions**

- Whisk together vanilla, brown sugar, and balsamic vinegar in a small mixing bowl.
- In a separate mixing bowl, combine the raspberries, blueberries, and strawberries. Add the vinegar mixture to the berries. Leave the fruit to marinate for ten to fifteen minutes. After that, drain the marinade.
- Serve immediately or refrigerate. To dish up, divide the berries into two serving dishes, and on the side of each, place the shortbread biscuit.

- Refrigerate or serve immediately. To serve, divide the berries into 2 serving dishes. Place the shortbread biscuit on the side of the bowl.

**Nutritional facts per serving**

**Serving size**: ¾ cup

Dietary fiber 4 g, Total carbohydrate 33 g, Calories 176, Monounsaturated fat Trace, Trans fat 0 g, Saturated fat 2 g, Total fat 4 g, Sodium 56 mg, Cholesterol 5 g, Added sugars 8 g.

# Chocolate Pudding Pies

These easy and quick pies make great snacks or desserts. The pies can be topped with cubed fresh fruits such as raspberries or strawberries instead of using sprinkles for garnish.

**Yield:** 6 Servings

**Ingredients**

- 1 packet (3 oz) of instant chocolate pudding
- 6 cracker crusts (each, 3 inches long)
- 6 tbsp of whipped topping
- 2 cups of skim milk
- Sprinkles, for garnish

**Directions**

- Combine the pudding and milk in a medium bowl. Whisk until well blended. Cover and place in the refrigerator for about 15 minutes, until the pudding thickens.
- Ladle ⅓ cup of pudding mixture into each of the graham cracker crusts. Top each with one tbsp of whipped topping and garnish with the sprinkles. Enjoy!

**Nutritional facts per serving**

**Serving size:** 1 pie

Total carbohydrate 30 g, Dietary fiber 0.5 g, Trans fat 0 g, Saturated fat 3 g, Monounsaturated fat 2 g, Total fat 5 g, Cholesterol 0.5 mg, Added sugars 18 g, Calories 175, Protein 4 g.

**Yield:** 3 Servings

High Fiber

Low Fat

**Ingredients**

- 6 chocolate wafer cookies, mashed
- 1⅓ cups of vanilla soy milk (soya milk), refrigerated
- 3 cups of fat-free vanilla ice cream

**Directions**

- Combine ice cream and soy milk in a blender. Puree until well blended and foamy. Add cookies to the soy milk mixture and pulse a few times to smooth. Pour into chilled glasses and dish up immediately.

**Nutritional facts per serving**

**Serving size:** 1 cup

Total carbohydrate 52 g, Trans fat 0 g, Saturated fat 1 g, Monounsaturated fat < 1 g, Total fat 3 g, Calories 270, Added sugars 11 g, Total sugars 29 g, Sodium 224 mg, Dietary fiber 11.5 g, Protein 9 g, Cholesterol Trace.

# Creamy Fruit Desserts

Ounce for ounce, mandarin oranges have about half the vitamin C that oranges do, but they have three times the vitamin A (carotene).

**Yield:** 4 Servings

Low Fat

Healthy carb

**Ingredients**

- ½ cup of plain fat-free yogurt
- 4 oz of fat-free cream cheese, softened
- ½ tsp of vanilla extract
- 1 tsp of sugar
- 1 can of (8 oz) water-packed pineapple chunks
- 1 can of (14.5 oz) water-packed sliced peaches
- 1 can of (15 oz) mandarin oranges
- 4 tbsp of toasted coconut, minced

**Directions**

- Add the cream cheese, vanilla, yogurt, and sugar in a small mixing bowl. Whisk until smooth with an electric mixer on high speed.
- Drain the canned fruits. Combine the pineapple, peaches, and oranges in another bowl. Pour the cream cheese mixture over the fruits mixture and stir to combine.

Cover the bowl and place in the refrigerator until chilled.

- To serve, place into individual serving cups and garnish with minced coconut. Enjoy.

**Nutritional facts per serving**

**Serving size**: About 1 cup

Dietary fiber 2 g, Cholesterol 3 mg, Calories 206, Trans fat 0 g, Saturated fat 1.5 g, Monounsaturated fat Trace, Total fat 2 g, Sodium 241 mg, Total carbohydrate 41 g, Added sugars 3 g, Total sugars 38 g, Protein 6 g.

# Lemon Zest Cheese

Lemon zest is alive with essential oils that add active aroma and flavor to this recipe. Grate the lemon with a hand-held grater to get the zest.

**Yield:** 8 Servings

Low Fat

**Ingredients**

- 1 envelope of unflavored gelatin
- 2 tbsp of lemon juice
- 2 tbsp of cold water
- 2 cups of low-fat cottage cheese
- Egg substitute equivalent to 2 egg whites or 1 egg
- ½ cup of skim milk, heated almost to boiling
- ¼ cup of sugar
- Lemon zest
- 1 tsp of vanilla

**Directions**

- In a blender, add the gelatin, lemon juice, and water. Blend on low speed for about 2 minutes for gelatin to be softened.
- Add the heated milk and blend until gelatin is dissolved. Add the vanilla, cheese, egg substitute, and sugar to the gelatin mixture. Blend on high speed until smooth

- Transfer into a round flat dish or 9-inch pie plate and place in the refrigerator for about 3 hours.

- To serve, top with the grated lemon zest if desired.

**Nutritional facts per serving**

**Serving size**: ⅛ of cake

Calories 80, Total carbohydrate 9 g, Trans fat 0 g, Dietary fiber Trace, Monounsaturated fat Trace, Saturated fat Trace, Total fat 1 g, Sodium 252 mg, Added sugars 9 g, Cholesterol 3 mg, Protein 9 g, Added sugars 9 g.

# Whole-Grain Coffeecake with Berries

**Yield:** 8 Servings

Low Sodium

**Ingredients**

- 1 cup of whole-wheat pastry flour
- ½ cup of skim milk
- 2 tbsp of canola oil
- 1 tbsp of vanilla
- 1 tbsp of vinegar
- ½ tsp of baking soda
- ½ tsp of ground cinnamon
- ⅓ cup of packed brown sugar
- ¼ cup of low-fat granola, slightly minced
- 1 egg
- ⅛ Tsp of salt
- 1 cup of frozen mixed berries, such as blackberries, raspberries, and blueberries (don't thaw)
- **Directions**
- Preheat the oven to 350°F temperatures. Get an 8-inch round cake pan, spray it with cooking spray, and use flour to coat it.

- Combine the milk, brown sugar, egg, oil, and vinegar in a large mixing bowl. Mix until well blended. Add flour, cinnamon, baking soda, and salt. Stir until moistened.

- And then, crease half the berries into the batter. Ladle the batter into the prepared pan. Sprinkle the mixture with the remaining berries and top it with granola.

- Place in the preheated oven and bake until golden brown, 25 to 30 minutes. When done, transfer the pan to a cooling rack and let it cool for 10 minutes. Dish up warm.

**Nutritional facts per serving**

**Serving size**: 1 slice

Sodium 139 mg, Cholesterol 23 mg, Dietary fiber 3 g, Calories 144, Trans fat Trace, Saturated fat 0.5 g, Monounsaturated fat 1.5 g, Total fat 4 g, Total carbohydrate 23 g, Added sugars 7 g, Protein 4.

# Rainbow Iced Pops

Fruit pops are a revitalizing dessert and an amusing way for adults and children to eat more fruit.

**Yield:** 6 Servings

Low Fat

Healthy carb

Low Sodium

**Ingredients**

- 1½ cups of diced watermelon, cantaloupe, and strawberries
- 2 cups of 100% apple juice
- ½ cup of blueberries
- 6 craft sticks
- 6 paper cups (6-8 oz each)

**Directions**

- Combine the fruit in a medium bowl and divide equally into the paper cups. Add the apple juice to each of the paper cups.
- Position the cups on a level surface inside the freezer. Let it freeze about 60 minutes or until partially frozen. Then, slot in a stick into the middle of each of the cups. Freeze the fruit until well frozen. Enjoy.

**Nutritional facts per serving**

**Serving size**: 1 pop

Calories 60, Sodium 6 mg, Total carbohydrate 14 g, Cholesterol 0 mg, Monounsaturated fat Trace, Saturated fat Trace, Total fat Trace, Dietary fiber 1 g, Added sugars 0 g, Protein 0.5 g, Total sugars 11 g.

# Delicious Apple Pie

**Yield:** 8 Servings

Healthy carb

Low Sodium

**Ingredients**

**For Pie crust**

- ¼ cup of whole-wheat pie flour
- 1 cup of dry rolled oats
- ¼ cup of ground almonds
- 3 tbsp of canola oil
- 2 tbsp of packed brown sugar
- 1 tbsp of water

**For Filling**

- 2 tbsp of quick-cooking tapioca
- ⅓ Cup of frozen apple juice concentrate
- 6 cups of peeled and sliced tart apples (approx 4 large apples)
- 1 tsp of cinnamon

**Directions**

- To make pie crust, in a large bowl, combine all the dry ingredients.

- In another container, whisk together the water and oil and add to the dry ingredients. Stir until dough holds together. If required, add a little extra water. In a 9-inch pie plate, press the dough and set aside

- To make the filling, in a large bowl, combine all the filling ingredients. Set aside for 15 minutes. Then stir and ladle into the pie crust mixture.

- Heat oven to 425°F and bake for 15 minutes. Then reduce the heat to 350°F and bake until apples are softened, for about 40 minutes.

**Nutritional facts per serving**

**Serving size:** 1 slice

Total carbohydrate 29 g, Sodium 2 mg, Calories 204, Cholesterol 0 mg, Monounsaturated fat 5 g, Trans fat Trace, Saturated fat 0.5 g, Total fat 8 g, Dietary fiber 4 g, Protein 4 g, Added sugars 3 g.

# Juicy Poached Pears

This awesome recipe is an excellent complement to any meal. Poaching involves simmering of ingredients on low heat, in a savory liquid or water. Pears are simmered in apple and orange juice in this recipe. The pears will still hold their shape.

**Yield: 4 Servings**

Low Sodium

Low Fat

**Ingredients**

- 4 whole pears
- 1 cup of orange juice
- 1 tsp of ground cinnamon
- 1 tsp of ground nutmeg
- ½ cup of fresh raspberries
- ¼ cup of apple juice
- 2 tbsp orange zest

**Directions**

- Combine the juices, nutmeg, and cinnamon in a small bowl. Stir to combine well.
- Take out the core from the pear's base, peel, but do not remove the stems. Put the pears inside a shallow pan. Pour the juice mixture over the pears and place over low heat. Simmer about thirty minutes, while frequently turning the pears. Do not boil.

- Move the pears to individual serving dishes. To serve, garnish with orange zest and raspberries.

**Nutritional facts per serving**

**Serving size:** 1 pear

Total carbohydrate 34 g, Sodium 9 mg, Total fat 0.5 g, Cholesterol 0 mg, Calories 140, Saturated fat Trace, Monounsaturated fat Trace, Trans fat 0 g, Dietary fiber 2 g, Added sugars 0 g, Protein 1 g.

# MAIN DISH RECIPES

# Baked Baguette with Blueberry

**Yield:** 5 Servings

Low Fat

**Ingredients**

- 12-inch sourdough baguette or French loaf
- ¾ cup of coarsely chopped blueberries
- 1 cup of fat-free soy milk
- 1 tbsp of canola oil
- 4 egg whites
- ¼ tsp of nutmeg
- ¼ cup of diced pecans
- 1 tsp of vanilla
- 4 tbsp of brown sugar, divided

**Directions**

- Coat a nine-inch square baking dish with cooking spray. Cut ten 1-inch chunky pieces from the baguette and arrange them hem in the baking dish.

- Whisk egg whites in a large container until foamy. Stir in vanilla, milk, 2 tbsp of sugar, and nutmeg.

- Pour the mixture evenly over the baguette ensuring the slices are well coated. Cover the dish overnight or no less than eight hours, until the mixture is soaked up by the baguette.

- Preheat the oven to a temperature of 400° F. And then place the chopped blueberries evenly over the baguette. Whisk the remaining 2 tbsp of brown sugar and oil together. If you wish, add the pecans.

- Ladle the sugar mixture evenly over bread. Place in the oven and bake until liquid from blueberries bubbling, about minutes. Serve immediately.

**Nutritional facts per serving**

Serving size: 2 slices

Total carbohydrate 30 g, Total carbohydrate 30 g, Calories 171, Cholesterol 0 mg, Sodium 249 mg, Monounsaturated fat 2 g, Trans fat 0 g, Saturated fat 0.5 g, Total fat 3 g, Added sugars 10 g, Protein 6 g, Dietary fiber 0.5 g.

# Wild Rice with Baked Chicken

**Yield:** 6 Servings

- Low Fat
- Low Sodium
- Healthy carb

**Ingredients**

- 1 pound of skinless, boneless chicken breast halves
- ¾ cup of uncooked wild rice
- ¾ cup of uncooked long-grain white rice
- 2 cups of unsalted chicken stock
- 1 ½ cups of whole pearl onions
- 1½ cups of sliced celery
- 1 tsp of fresh tarragon
- 1 ½ cups of dry white wine

**Directions**

- Preheat the oven to 300° F temperature and then cut the chicken breast into 1-inch pieces.
- Combine chicken, onions, celery, and tarragon with one cup of the chicken stock in a nonstick frying pan. Place on medium heat and cook about 10 minutes or until the chicken and veggies are softened. Leave to cool.

- Combine the rice, reaming one cup of chicken stock and wine in a baking dish. Leave to marinate for 3 minutes.
- Add the vegetables and chicken to the baking dish. Cover and bake in the preheated oven for 60 minutes. Check occasionally and add additional stock if the rice is too dry. Serve hot.

**Nutritional facts per serving**

Serving size: About 1 ½ cups

Cholesterol 55 mg, Sodium 104 mg, Total carbohydrate 38 g, Dietary fiber 2.5 g, Monounsaturated fat 1 g, Saturated fat 1 g, Trans fat Trace, Total fat 3 g, Added sugars 0 g, Calories 313, Total sugars 2 g, Protein 23 g.

# French-Loaf Pizza

Bake in a pizza stone to get a crispier pizza. For best results, place the pizza on the lowest shelf of the oven.

**Yield: 4 Servings**

**Ingredients**

- 1 cup of cubed red bell pepper
- 1 cup of cubed Roma tomatoes
- 1 cup of cubed asparagus
- 1 cup of pizza sauce
- 1 tbsp of crushed garlic
- 1 cup of low-fat grated mozzarella cheese
- 1 loaf of French bread, approx 8 inches in diameter, sliced in half and cut into 4-inch pieces

**Directions**

- Preheat the oven to 400° F temperature. Lightly spray a baking sheet with cooking spray.
- Combine the asparagus, pepper, and tomatoes in a small bowl. Then add garlic and mix softly to combine well.
- Place the French bread on the prepared baking sheet. Add ¼ cup of the veggie mixture and ¼ cup of the pizza sauce to each piece.
- After that, sprinkle each slice of bread with ¼ cup of mozzarella cheese.

- Place in the preheated oven and bake for about 10 minutes, until the cheese is a bit browned. Dish up immediately.

**Nutritional facts per serving**

Serving size: 1 4-inch section

Total carbohydrate 40 g, Dietary fiber 4 g, Sodium 660 mg, Calories 265, Monounsaturated fat 0.5 g, Trans fat 0 g, Saturated fat 2 g, Total fat 5 g, Protein 15 g, Cholesterol 12 mg, Added sugars 0 g.

# Baked Macaroni with Spaghetti Sauce

**Yield:** 6 Servings

- Low Sodium
- High Fiber
- Healthy carb

**Ingredients**

- 1 box (7 oz) of whole-wheat elbow macaroni
- 1 small onion, chopped (approx. ½ cup)
- ½ pound of extra-lean ground beef
- 6 tbsp of Parmesan cheese
- 1 jar (15 oz) of low-sodium spaghetti sauce

**Directions**

- Preheat the oven to a temperature of 350° F. and spray a baking plate with cooking spray.
- Boil the ground beef and onion in a non-stick frying pan until the onion is translucent and meat is browned. Set aside.
- Pour water ¾ full into a large saucepot and bring to a boil over medium heat. Add pasta and boil according to package instructions or for about 12 minutes. After that, drain the pasta well
- Add the boiled pasta and spaghetti sauce to the cooked meat. Stir to combine well. In the prepared baking dish,

ladle the mixture and bake in the preheated oven for approx 25 to 35 minutes or until bubbly.

- When done, transfer the macaroni into the individual plates. Sprinkle each of the plates with one tbsp of parmesan cheese. Serve instantly.

**Nutritional facts per serving**

**Serving size**: About 1 cup

Total carbohydrate 32 g, Cholesterol 32 mg, Dietary fiber 4 g, Sodium 125 mg, Calories 269, Monounsaturated fat 3 g, Trans fat Trace, Saturated fat 3 g, Total fat 9 g, Saturated fat 3 g, Total sugars 6 g, Added sugars 0 g, Protein 15 g

# Mealtime Burrito

You can use egg white for this recipe if you do not have an egg substitute.

**Yield:** 2 Servings

High Fiber

Low Fat

Healthy carb

**Ingredients**

- 2 whole-wheat tortillas, 6 inches' long
- ½cup of frozen corn
- 4 tbsp of diced onion
- 1 cup of chopped tomato
- 2 tbsp of salsa
- ½cup of egg substitute (or 4 egg whites)

**Directions**

- Combine the corn, tomato, and onion in a small frying pan. Place over medium heat and cook until moisture has gone, and vegetables are tender. Stir in the egg substitute or egg whites to the vegetables and cook about 3 minutes until cooked through.
- To serve, place each tortilla in a serving dish and spread the vegetable mixture evenly in the middle of each. Fold in the two sides of each tortilla up over the vegetable mixture and roll to close. Dish up immediately.

### Nutritional facts per serving

**Serving size:** 1 burrito

Total carbohydrate 30 g, Sodium 370 mg, Cholesterol 1 mg, Trans fat 0 g, Monounsaturated fat Trace, Saturated fat Trace, Total fat 1 g, Calories 173, Added sugars 0 g, Total sugars 4 g, Dietary fiber 12 g, Protein 11 g.

# Sesame and Ginger Shrimps

**Yield:** 6 Servings

Healthy carb

**Ingredients**

- 12 oz shrimp, peeled and deveined
- 6 tbsp of reduced-sodium soy sauce
- 4 garlic cloves, crushed
- 2 tbsp of freshly crushed ginger
- 2 tbsp of sesame oil
- 1 tsp of red pepper flakes
- 2 ½ tbsp of brown sugar

**Directions**

- Combine the soy sauce, garlic, ginger, red pepper flakes, brown sugar, and oil in a medium bowl. Add the shrimp and mix to combine. Refrigerate for 30 minutes to marinate.
- Lightly spray a nonstick sauté pan with cooking spray. Place the pan over medium heat; add the shrimp and sauté for 60 seconds. Add half of the marinated mixture and heat for an additional 30 seconds. Dispose of the remaining marinade. Enjoy.

**Nutritional facts per serving**

Serving size: 2 oz per serving

Total carbohydrate 6 g, Cholesterol 71 mg, Sodium 970 mg, Calories 108, Monounsaturated fat 2 g, Trans fat 0 g, Saturated fat 1 g, Total fat 5 g, Total sugars 4 g, Protein 9 g, Dietary fiber 0 g.

# Tasty Asian Pork Tenderloin

Serve this recipe with water chestnuts and steamed pea pods, fresh mango, papaya, and brown rice.

**Yield:** 4 Servings

Low Sodium

**Ingredients**

- 2 tbsp of sesame seeds
- ⅛ Tsp of cayenne pepper
- ⅛ Tsp of celery seed
- 1 tsp of ground coriander
- ⅛ Tsp of ground cinnamon
- ½ tsp of chopped onion
- ¼ tsp of ground cumin
- 1 tbsp of sesame oil
- 1 pound of pork tenderloin, cut into 4 pieces

**Directions**

- Preheat the oven to 400° F temperature. Spray a baking dish with cooking spray.
- Place the sesame seeds in a single layer in a nonstick frying pan. Heat the seeds over low heat for about 2 minutes, frequently stirring until golden brown. Take out the seeds from the pot and set aside to cool.

- Combine the coriander, cinnamon, celery seed, cayenne pepper, sesame oil, cumin, chopped onion, and roasted sesame seeds in a large bowl. Stir to combine well.

- Arrange the pork in the baking dish and rub the mixed ingredients on the two sides of each pork piece. Bake in the preheated oven for about 15 to 20 minutes until pork is no longer pink. Enjoy.

**Nutritional facts per serving**

**Serving size:** 1 piece

Cholesterol 73 mg, Sodium 61 mg, Total carbohydrate 1 g, Calories 176, Monounsaturated fat 3 g, Trans fat Trace, Saturated fat 2 g Total fat 8 g, Dietary fiber 0 g, Added sugars 0 g, Total sugars 0 g, Protein 25 g

# Whole-Wheat Blueberry Pancakes

**Yield**: 6 Servings

Healthy carb

Low Fat

**Ingredients**

- 2 tsp of baking powder
- 1 ⅓ cup of white whole-wheat flour
- ½ tsp of cinnamon
- 1 tbsp of sugar
- 1 ⅓ cup of skim milk
- 1 tbsp of canola oil
- 1 egg, lightly beaten
- 1 cup frozen or fresh whole blueberries

**Directions**

- Combine flour, sugar, baking powder, and cinnamon in a large bowl.
- Whisk together egg, milk, and oil in a separate bowl. Combine the egg mixture with flour mixture. Stir until flour is moistened.
- After that, add the blueberries and stir softly.
- Spray a skillet or griddle with cooking spray and place on medium-high heat. Pour approximately ¼ cup of the

mixture into hot skillet. And then cook one side until browned and then turn to brown the other side.

- Repeat to with the remaining batter.

**Nutritional facts per serving**

**Serving size**: 2 pancakes

Total carbohydrate 28 g, Dietary fiber 4 g, Cholesterol 35 mg, Trans fat 0 g, Monounsaturated fat 2 g, Saturated fat 1 g, Total fat 4 g, Calories 158, Added sugars 7 g, Sodium 240 mg, Protein 6 g.

# Smoky Frittata

If smoke Gouda is not available, add ¼ tsp of liquid smoke to regular Gouda cheese.

**Yield:** 6 Servings

Healthy carb

**Ingredients**

- ½ cup of grated smoked Gouda cheese
- ¼ cup of grated 2% sharp cheddar cheese
- 1 small head cauliflower, sliced into medium florets
- ¼ cup of light sour cream
- 2 tbsp of Dijon mustard
- 3 tbsp of thinly chopped chives
- 2 tsp of paprika
- 6 eggs
- ¼ tsp of ground black pepper
- ¼ tsp of salt
- 1 tsp of olive oil

**Directions**

- Preheat the oven to 375° F temperature. Add salted water to a large saucepan and simmer the cauliflower over low heat for about 5 minutes or until half-cooked. Remove from the heat source, drain, and dry cauliflower.

- Combine the sour cream, paprika, mustard, and eggs in a large mixing bowl. Stir until well combined. While stirring, add chives, ¾ of each cheese, pepper, and salt.

- Heat the olive oil in a large baking dish over medium heat, add cauliflower and fry about 5 minutes, or until one side is golden brown. Add the egg mixture to the cauliflower and cook for another 5 minutes.

- After that, sprinkle the mixture with the remaining cheese and move the pan to the preheated oven. Heat for about 12 minutes until the frittata is done. Leave for about 3 minutes to cool.

- To serve, cut into six wedges. Enjoy.

**Nutritional facts per serving**

**Serving size:** 1 wedge

Dietary fiber 2 g, Total carbohydrate 5 g, Calories 163, Monounsaturated fat 3 g, Trans fat 0 g, Saturated fat 5 g, Total fat 11 g, Sodium 467 mg, Total sugars 1 g, Cholesterol 199 mg, Protein 11 g.

# Yummy Tacos with Vegetables

Serve with Spanish rice, a green salad, and cantaloupe.

**Yield:** 4 Servings

Healthy carb

High Fiber

**Ingredients**

- 1 cup chopped green zucchini
- 1 medium red onion, sliced
- 3 large garlic cloves, crushed
- 4 medium tomatoes, seeded and sliced (approx 2 cups)
- 1 tbsp of olive oil
- 8 whole-wheat tortillas
- 1 jalapeno chili, seeded and minced
- 1 cup of cubed yellow summer squash
- 1 cup of fresh or frozen corn kernels
- 1 cup of canned black beans or pinto, washed and drained
- ½ cup of smoke-flavored salsa
- ½ cup of sliced fresh cilantro

**Directions**

- Heat olive oil in a large saucepot over medium heat. Once the oil is hot, add onion and cook until tender. Add the zucchini and summer squash. Cook about 5 minutes until soft. Add the tomatoes, corn, garlic, beans, and jalapeno. Cook for about 5 minutes until the veggies are soft, stirring occasionally. Add the cilantro and remove from the heat source.

- Place a large saucepan over medium heat. Add one tortilla to the pot and cook until tender, for about 20 seconds per side. Do the same to the remaining tortillas.

- T o serve, share the tortillas among individual serving. Spoon the vegetable mixture evenly on the tortillas and top each with 2 tbsp of the salsa.

**Nutritional facts per serving**

**Serving size**: 2 tacos

Total carbohydrate 55 g, Sodium 259 mg, Cholesterol 0 mg, Monounsaturated fat 3 g, Trans fat 0 g, Saturated fat 1 g, Total fat 4 g, Calories 300, Added sugars 0 g, Total sugars 8 g, Dietary fiber 26 g, Protein 11 g.

# Thai Peanut Beef Tenderloin

The thickness of your meat will determine the cooking time. You can use chicken in place of beef.

**Yield:** 2 Servings

**Ingredients**

- 5 tbsp of soy sauce
- 8 oz of beef tenderloin, rinsed and cut into 1oz pieces
- 2 tbsp of brown sugar
- 2 tbsp of creamy peanut butter
- 2 tbsp of chopped cilantro
- 2 tbsp of chopped scallions
- 1 tbsp of ginger powder
- 1 tbsp of vinegar
- ½ tsp of red pepper flakes
- ¼ tsp of salt
- 1 tbsp of sesame oil

**Directions**

- Combine the soy sauce, cilantro, sugar, peanut butter, red pepper flakes, ginger powder, scallions, and salt in a small mixing bowl. Whisk to combine well. Add beef to the soy sauce mixture and place in the refrigerator to marinate for not less than 30 minutes.

- Place a medium sauté pot over medium heat and add oil. When the pot is hot, add beef and let cook on both sides for about ten minutes. Add the remaining marinade to the pot. Reduce heat and cook until marinade is a bit thickened.

**Nutritional facts per serving**

**Serving size**: 4 oz beef with 3 tbsp of sauce

Total carbohydrate 10 g, Cholesterol 57 mg, Calories 307, Monounsaturated fat 7 g, Trans fat 0 g, Saturated fat 6 g, Total fat 19 g, Dietary fiber 1 g, Total sugars 7 g, Sodium 573 mg, Protein 27 g.

# Vegetarian Tofu with Chili

You can also serve warm chili with cornbread and chopped pears drizzled with nutmeg and cinnamon.

**Yield:** 4 Servings

Healthy carb

High Fiber

**Ingredients**

- 1 tbsp of olive oil
- 1 small yellow onion, sliced (about ½cup)
- 2 cans (14 oz each) of chopped, unsalted tomatoes
- 12 oz of extra-firm tofu, cut into bits
- 1 can (14 oz) of unsalted black, rinsed and drained
- 1 can (14 oz) of unsalted kidney beans, rinsed and drained
- 3 tbsp of chili powder
- 1 tbsp of sliced fresh cilantro
- 1 tbsp of oregano

**Directions**

- Place a saucepan over medium heat, add the olive oil. Once hot, add onions and sauté for about 6 minutes until onions are tender. Add the beans, tomatoes, tofu, oregano, and chili powder. Allow it to boil. And then reduce heat to low and simmer about 30 minutes. Take it out of heat source and stir in cilantro. Serve immediately.

**Nutritional facts per serving**

**Serving size**: About 2 cups

Total carbohydrate 46 g, Dietary fiber 16 g, Calories 314, Cholesterol 0 mg, Monounsaturated fat 3 g, Trans fat 0 g, Saturated fat 1 g, Total fat 6 g, Added sugars 0 g, Total sugars 10 g, Sodium 364 mg, Protein 19 g.

# White chicken-chili

For additional flavor, add more vegetables or add different types of beans, such as black or kidney beans. Just remember to add more chicken stock to contain the added ingredients.

**Yield:** 8 Servings

Low Fat

High Fiber

Healthy carb

**Ingredients**

- 1 can (10 oz) of white chunk chicken
- 1 can (14.5 oz) of reduced-sodium chopped tomatoes
- 2 cans (15 oz each) of reduced-sodium white beans rinse and drained
- 4 cups of reduced-sodium chicken stock
- 8 tbsp of grated low-fat Monterey Jack cheese
- 1 medium onion, sliced
- 1 medium red pepper, sliced
- ½ medium green pepper, sliced
- 2 garlic cloves, crushed
- 2 tsp of chili powder
- 1 tsp of dried oregano

- 1 tsp of ground cumin
- Cayenne pepper, to taste
- 3 tbsp of sliced fresh cilantro

**Directions**

- Combine the chicken, tomatoes, beans, and chicken stock in a large saucepot. Place the pot over medium heat, and simmer covered about 15 minutes.
- Coat a non-stick frying pan with cooking spray and then add onions, garlic, and peppers. Sauté the vegetables until tender, about 5 minutes,
- Spoon the vegetable mixture to the saucepot. Stir in the oregano, cumin, chili powder, and cayenne pepper. Simmer on low heat until all the veggies are tender, about 10 minutes.
- Transfer to individual serving dishes. Sprinkle each of the servings with 1 tbsp of cheese and garnish with cilantro.

**Nutritional facts per serving**

**Serving size**: About 1½cups

Total carbohydrate 25 g, Cholesterol 27 mg, Calories 212, Monounsaturated fat 1 g, Trans fat 0 g, Saturated fat 1.5 g, Total fat 4 g, Sodium 241 mg, Added sugars 0 g, Total sugars 4 g, Dietary fiber 6 g, Protein 19 g.

# Grilled Asian Salmon

**Yield: 4 Servings**

Low Sodium

**Ingredients**

- 1 tbsp of low-sodium soy sauce
- 1 tbsp of sesame oil
- 4 salmon fillets, 4 oz each
- 1 tbsp of rice wine vinegar
- 1 tbsp of fresh ginger, crushed

**Directions**

- Combine soy sauce, sesame oil, vinegar, and ginger in a shallow glass bowl. Add salmon to the soy sauce mixture and turn to coat all sides. Place in the refrigerator for about 1 hour while turning infrequently.
- Coat the grill with oil and place over medium-high heat. Add salmon to the grill and cook each side for 5 minutes or fork or knife can enter the fish quickly. Serve warm.

**Nutritional facts per serving**

**Serving size**: One fillet

Total carbohydrate 1 g, Sodium 113 mg, Calories 185, Cholesterol 57 mg, Monounsaturated fat 3 g, Trans fat Trace, Saturated fat 2 g, Total fat 9 g, Added sugars 0 g, Dietary fiber Trace, Protein 26 g.

# Pasta Salad Mixed with Vegetables

Any shape of pasta can be used for this salad, and for a different variety, you can try carrot, tomato, or spinach-flavored pasta.

**Yield:** 8 Servings

High Fiber

Low Sodium

Healthy carb

Low Fat

- **Ingredients**
- 12 oz of whole-wheat pasta
- ¼ cup of reduced-sodium chicken stock
- 1 can (28 oz) of unsalted cubed tomatoes in juice
- 1 tbsp of olive oil
- 1 garlic clove, minced
- 1 pound of mushrooms, sliced
- 1 green bell pepper, chopped
- 1 red bell pepper, chopped
- 2 medium onions, sliced
- 8 romaine lettuce leaves
- 2 medium zucchini, grated
- 2 tsp of oregano

- ½ tsp of basil

**Directions**

- Boil the pasta following the package directions. Drain and put the pasta in a large container, add olive oil, toss to combine, and set aside.

- Pour the chicken stock into a large fry pan. Place the pan over medium heat and add tomatoes, onions, and garlic. Sauté until onions are tender and translucent, approx 5 minutes. After that, add the remaining veggies and sauté for another 5 minutes until soft. Stir in the oregano and basil.

Add the sautéed vegetable mixture to the pasta and toss to combine well. Cover and place in the refrigerator to chill about 60 minutes.

To serve, put lettuce leaves on each of the serving dishes. Top with the pasta salad. Enjoy.

**Nutritional facts per serving**

**Serving size:** About 2 cups

Calories 251, Cholesterol Trace, Total carbohydrate 46 g, Dietary fiber 8 g, Trans fat 0 g, Monounsaturated fat 1.5 g, Saturated fat 0.5 g, Total fat 3 g, Sodium 60 mg, Added sugars 0 g, Total sugars 10 g, Protein 10 g.

# SALAD RECIPES

# Julienned Vegetables Salad

Cut the vegetables of this recipe into thin strips to create an attractive appearance.

**Yield:** 4 Servings

Serves 4

Healthy carb

**Ingredients**

- ½ cup of julienned red bell pepper
- 1 ½ cup of julienned carrot
- ½ cup of julienned yellow onion
- 1 ½ cup of julienned bok choy
- 1 ½ cup of finely sliced spinach
- 1 cup of finely sliced red cabbage
- 1 tbsp of finely sliced cilantro
- 1 ½ tbsp of minced cashews
- 1 tbsp of crushed garlic
- 1 ½ cups of snow peas
- 2 tsp of reduced-sodium soy sauce

- 2 tsp of toasted sesame oil

**Directions**

- Under cold running water, rinse all the vegetables. Drain after rinsing. Cut the carrot, onion, bok choy, and pepper into skinny strips. Also, cut the cabbage, cilantro, and spinach across the grain into thin strips.
- Then, toss all the cut vegetables together with snow peas, cashew, and garlic in a large bowl. Sprinkle soy sauce and sesame oil over the salad and then toss again to combine well. Enjoy.

**Nutritional facts per serving**

**Serving size**: approx 2 cups

Calories 113, Dietary fiber 4 g, Total carbohydrate 14 g, Cholesterol 0 mg, Sodium 168 mg, Monounsaturated fat 2 g, Trans fat 0 g, Saturated fat 1 g, Total fat 4 g, Added sugars 0 g, Total sugars 6 g, Protein 3 g

# Apple Salad with Almonds and Figs

Figs are rich in calcium, phosphorus, and iron. You can add figs to baked goods or eat them raw, as it is in this salad.

**Yield:** 6 Servings

Low Sodium

Low Fat

Healthy carb

**Ingredients**

- 6 dried figs, sliced (approx. 1 cup)
- 2 big red apples, cored and cubed (approx. 4 cups)
- 2 ribs of celery, cubed (approx. 2 cups)
- 2 carrots, peeled and shredded (approx. ¾ cup)
- 2 tbsp of slivered almonds
- ½ cup of fat-free lemon yogurt

**Directions**

- Combine figs, apple, celery, and carrots in a medium bowl. Add in yogurt and mix to combine. Top with the slivered almonds. Enjoy.

**Nutritional facts per serving**

**Serving size**: approx. 1 cup

Calories 93, Cholesterol Trace, Sodium 33 mg, Total carbohydrate 19 g, Dietary fiber 3 g, Monounsaturated fat 1 g,

Trans fat 0 g, Saturated fat Trace, Total fat 1 g, Added sugars 0 g, Total sugars 14 g, Protein 2 g.

# Spinach and Blue Cheese Salad

If you wish, lightly toast the sliced walnut in a small frying pan to increase their flavor.

**Yield:** 12 Servings

- Healthy carb
- Low Sodium
- Low Fat

**Ingredients**

**For dressing:**

- 2 tbsp of balsamic vinegar
- 4 tsp of olive oil
- 1 tbsp plain low-fat yogurt
- ¼ tsp of nutmeg
- 1 tbsp of maple syrup

**For salad:**

- 2 pounds spinach, coarsely chopped (or 3 10-oz packages)
- 1 ½ cups chopped cucumber
- ½ cup of chopped red onion
- ¼ cup of sliced walnuts
- 1 ½ cups of grape tomatoes
- ¼ cup of blue cheese crumbles

## Directions

- Blend all the ingredients for dressing in a food processor or blender. Refrigerate until chilled.
- After that, toss the dressing with spinach greens and knoll 2 cups onto chilled serving dishes.
- Spread the vegetables, blue cheese crumbles, and walnuts over the spinach. Enjoy.

## Nutritional facts per serving

**Serving size**: 2 ½ cups

Calories 70, Cholesterol 2 mg, Total carbohydrate 7 g, Sodium 95 mg, Dietary fiber 2 g, Monounsaturated fat 2 g, Trans fat 0 g, Saturated fat 1 g, Total fat 4 g, Added sugars 1 g, Protein 4 g, Total sugars 2.5 g.

# Apple and Butternut Squash Salad

If desired, you can toast butter squash to intensify the flavor of this recipe.

**Yield:** 6 Servings

High Fiber

Low Sodium

Low Fat

Healthy carb

**Ingredients**

- 1 butternut squash, peeled, seeded, and cut into ½-inch pieces (approx. 8 cups)
- 2 tsp of olive oil
- 2 large apples, cored and cut ½-inch pieces
- 6 cups of chopped spinach
- 1 ½ cups of sliced celery
- 2 cups of minced carrots
- 6 cups of chopped arugula

**For dressing:**

- 2 tsp of balsamic vinegar
- ½ cup of reduced-fat plain yogurt
- 1½ tsp of honey

## Directions

- Preheat the oven to 400° F temperature.
- Toss together squash and olive oil in a baking dish. Roast in the preheated oven for about 30 minutes until squash tender and golden brown. Set aside to coll.
- In a large bowl, combine all the vegetables and the roasted squash.
- To prepare the dressing, combine vinegar, yogurt, and honey in a small bowl. Mix until well combined. Then top the dressing on the salad and toss. Serve immediately.

## Nutritional facts per serving

**Serving size**: About 4 cups

Total carbohydrate 42 g, Cholesterol 1 mg, Sodium 96 mg, Calories 215, Monounsaturated fat 1 g, Trans fat 0 g, Saturated fat 1 g, Total fat 3 g, Added sugars 1 g, Dietary fiber 8 g, Protein 5 g.

# Delicious Crab Salad

**Yield**: 4 Servings

Low Fat

**Ingredients**

- ¼ cup of rice wine vinegar
- ¼ cup of lime juice
- 1 tsp of sugar
- ⅓ Cup of chopped fresh mint
- 1 cucumber, seeded and finely chopped
- 12 oz of cooked, drained crab meat
- 4 cups of mixed romaine lettuce or salad greens
- 4 lime wedges

**Directions**

- Combine the vinegar, lime juice, cucumber, mint and, sugar in a medium bowl. Add the crab to the mixture and toss it to be well coated.
- Share the lettuce among individual serving dishes and spoon the crab mixture on top. Ladle the remaining dressing on top of the crab. Garnish with lime wedges. Enjoy.

**Nutritional facts per serving**

**Serving size**: 1 cup of lettuce with ½ cup of crab dressing

Calories 121 g, Dietary fiber 2 g, Total carbohydrate 11 g, Trans fat 1 g, Saturated fat < 1 g, Monounsaturated fat < 1 g, Total fat 1 g, Cholesterol 50 mg, Added sugars 1 g, Sodium 304 mg, Protein 17 g.

# Assorted Beans Salad

**Yield:** 8 Servings

Healthy carb

High Fiber

Low Fat

**Ingredients**

- 1 can (15 oz) of unsalted garbanzo beans
- 1 can (15 oz) of unsalted kidney beans
- 1 can (15 oz) of unsalted wax beans
- 1 can (15 oz) of unsalted green beans
- ¼ cup of finely sliced white onion
- ¼ cup of cider vinegar
- ¼cup of orange juice
- Sugar substitute, if desired

**Directions**

- Rinse and drain all the beans. Add the beans and onion in a large bowl. Mix gently to combine well.
- Mix the vinegar and orange juice in another bowl. If you wish, add sugar substitute to your taste.
- Add the orange juice mixture to the bean mixture. Toss to combine well. Serve after 30 minutes.

**Nutritional facts per serving**

**Serving size**: ¾ cup (generous)

Sodium 165 mg, Cholesterol 0 mg, Monounsaturated fat Trace, Trans fat 0 g, Saturated fat Trace, Total fat 2 g, Calories 126, Total carbohydrate 21 g, Added sugars 0 g, Dietary fiber 6 g, Protein 7 g.

# Flavored Melon Salad

This recipe is a perfect way to enjoy fruit at every meal. It is excellent for breakfast, lunch as well as dessert

**Yield:** 4 Servings

Healthy carb

Low Fat

Low Sodium

**Ingredients**

- 2 cups of cubed assorted melon, such as watermelon, honeydew or cantaloupe (or any fruit of your choice)
- ½ cup of vanilla or plain non-fat or low-fat yogurt
- ¼ tsp of nutmeg
- ⅛Tsp of clove
- ¼ tsp of mace
- ⅛Tsp of cinnamon
- 3tbsp of orange juice
- 1 tbsp of orange zest

**Directions**

- Add all the ingredients in a large bowl and mix to combine well. Enjoy.

**Nutritional facts per serving**

**Serving size**: About ½ cup

Total carbohydrate 11 g, Cholesterol 1 mg, Calories 52, Monounsaturated fat Trace, Trans fat 0 g, Saturated fat Trace, Total fat Trace, Dietary fiber 1 g, Added sugars 0 g, Sodium 31 mg, Protein 2 g.

# Spiced Potato Salad

This low-fat low-sodium potato salad recipe is tastier and healthier.

**Yield**: 8 Servings

Low Fat

Low Sodium

Healthy carb

**Ingredients**

- 1 pound of potatoes, cubed and steamed or boiled
- 1 cup of chopped yellow onion
- ½ cup of diced carrot
- ½ cup of diced celery
- 2 tbsp of crushed fresh dill or ½ tbsp dried
- ¼ cup of low-calorie mayonnaise
- 1 tsp of ground black pepper
- 2 tbsp of red wine vinegar
- 1 tbsp of Dijon mustard

**Directions**

- Add all the ingredients in a large bowl and mix to combine well. Serve when chilled.

**Nutritional facts per serving**

**Serving size**: About ¾ cup

Cholesterol 2 mg, Calories 77, Total carbohydrate 14 g, Dietary fiber 2 g, Monounsaturated fat < 0.5 g Trans fat 0 g, Saturated fat Trace, Total fat 1 g, Sodium 127 mg, Total sugars 2 g, Added sugars 0 g, Protein 1 g.

# SANDWICH RECIPES

# Turkey and Vegetable Wrap

**Yield:** 4 Servings

Healthy carb

**Ingredients**

- 12 oz of chopped deli turkey (reduced-sodium)
- ¼ cup of salsa
- ¼ cup of avocado
- ½ cup of finely chopped carrots
- 1 cup of grated green cabbage
- ½ cup of chopped tomatoes
- 2 whole-wheat tortillas (12-inch long

**Directions**

- Add the avocado and salsa in a small bowl and mix well to combine. Cover and refrigerate for about 30 minutes. Combine the turkey, carrots, cabbage, and tomatoes in a separate bowl.
- After that, spoon the avocado salsa evenly over two tortillas. Divide the turkey mixture among the tortillas. Fold each side of the tortillas up to cover the filling. Roll to close and then cut each in half. Serve immediately.

**Nutritional facts per serving**

**Serving size**: ½ wrap

Total carbohydrate 15 g, Cholesterol 59 mg, Calories 226, Monounsaturated fat 3 g, Trans fat Trace, Saturated fat 2 g, Total fat 6 g, Added sugars 0 g, Dietary fiber 4 g, Sodium 253 mg, Protein 28 g.

# Tuna Salad Sandwich

For variety, add tomato or cucumber slices, fresh chives, raisins or diced apples to each sandwich. Make use of unsalted can tuna to reduce sodium as fat-free mayonnaise increases sodium.

**Yield:** 4 Servings

Healthy carb

**Ingredients**

- 2 cans (6 oz each) no-salt white tuna packed in water and drained
- 8 slices whole-wheat bread
- ½ cup of chopped celery
- 1 tsp of lemon juice
- ⅓ Cup of fat-free mayonnaise
- 4 lettuce leaves

**Directions**

- In a small bowl, add the tuna and flake with a fork. Add celery, mayonnaise, and lemon juice and combine.
- To serve, put one lettuce leaf on a slice of bread. Spoon ¼ of the tuna mixture on it and place another slice of bread on top. Do the same to the remaining slices. Enjoy.

**Nutritional facts per serving**

**Serving size:** 1 sandwich

Cholesterol 38 mg, Dietary fiber 4 g, Calories 253, Total carbohydrate 25 g, Trans fat Trace, Monounsaturated fat 1 g, Saturated fat 1 g, Total fat 5 g, Sodium 445 mg, Added sugars 0 g, Total sugars 4 g, Protein 27 g.

# Basil and Tomato Sandwich

Pita bread is very popular in the Mediterranean regions and the Middle East.

**Yield** 2 Servings

Healthy carb

**Ingredients**

- 1 whole-wheat pita bread, sliced into 2
- 2 oz of low-fat smoked provolone cheese
- 6 fresh basil leaves
- 2 leaves of romaine lettuce
- ½ of small red onions, finely sliced
- 1 finely chopped tomato
- Freshly ground black pepper
- ½ tsp of balsamic vinegar

**Directions**

In a toaster, toast the bread halves and open the insides. Divide the basil, lettuce, cheese, tomato, and onion and layer between the two pitas. Sprinkle with the ground pepper and balsamic vinegar. Enjoy.

**Nutritional facts per serving**

**Serving size:** Half pita

Total carbohydrate 23 g, Dietary fiber 3 g, Calories 199, Cholesterol 15 mg, Monounsaturated fat 0 g, Trans fat 0 g, Saturated fat 4 g, Total fat 7 g, Added sugars 0 g, Sodium 311 mg, Protein 11 g.

# Coleslaw and Chicken Wrap

You can substitute plain roasted chicken breast (skinless and boneless) for canned chicken. This will reduce the sodium by approximately 25 percent.

**Yield:** 2 Servings

Healthy carb

High Fiber

**Ingredients**

**For the dressing:**

- 1 tbsp of olive oil
- ¼ tsp of celery or caraway seeds
- 2 tbsp of apple cider vinegar
- ½ tsp of sugar

**For the wraps:**

- 1 cup of grated cabbage (or packaged coleslaw mix without dressing)
- 1 can (5 oz) of chunky white meat chicken
- 2 whole-grain tortillas, 8 inches long each
- 1 can (4 oz) of minced pineapple, drained

**Directions**

- Combine the dressing al the dressing ingredients with chicken, pineapple, and cabbage in a medium bowl.

Cover and place inside the refrigerator for about 25 minutes.

- To serve, share the chicken dressing among the tortillas. Fold each side of the tortillas up to cover the filling. Fold to close and serve. Enjoy.

**Nutritional facts per serving**

**Serving size**: 1 wrap

Sodium 475 mg, Total carbohydrate 26 g, Trans fat 0 g, Saturated fat 2 g, Monounsaturated fat 8 g, Calories 324, Dietary fiber 13 g, Added sugars 2 g, Total sugars 8 g, Cholesterol 47 mg, Protein 25 g.

# Chicken Burritos

**Yield: 4 Servings**

Healthy carb

High Fiber

**Ingredients**

- 1 tsp of oil
- 1 jalapeno pepper, seed removed and finely sliced
- 1 red bell pepper, finely sliced
- 2 ribs celery, finely sliced
- 1 yellow onion, finely sliced
- 2 tbsp of cumin seed
- 1 pint (2 cups) of grape tomatoes
- 2 tbsp of fresh oregano
- 2 cloves garlic, finely sliced
- 4 whole-wheat tortillas (10-inch long each)
- 8 oz of cooked chicken breast
- 2 cups of grated green cabbage
- ½ cup of canned (unsalted) black beans, rinsed and drained

**Directions**

- Place a large frying pan over medium-high heat. Pour oil and sauté celery, peppers, cumin, and onion for about 15 minutes or until lightly brown. Add oregano, tomatoes, and garlic. Keep cooking until tomatoes blister and open, approx ten minutes. Move the sautéed ingredients to a blender and blend until smooth.
- Divide the chicken breast among the tortillas; add bean and cabbage and then top with the tomato sauce.

**Nutritional facts per serving**

**Serving size**: 1 burrito

Calories 286, Cholesterol 41 mg, Total carbohydrate 38 g, Trans fat Trace, Monounsaturated fat 3 g, Saturated fat 1 g, Sodium 382 mg, Dietary fiber 9 g, Total fat 6 g, Added sugars 0 g, Total sugars 9 g, Protein 20 g.

# SIDES RECIPES

# Glazed Root Vegetables

You can use any type of root vegetable to prepare this recipe. For variety, use parsnips, sweet potatoes, or rutabagas.

**Yield:** 4 Servings

Low Fat

Low Sodium

Healthy carb

**Ingredients**

- 1 ½ cups of water
- 1 tsp of olive oil
- ½ cup diced onions
- ½ cup diced parsnips
- ½ cup diced fresh potatoes
- ½ cup diced fresh carrots
- 2 tsp of sugar

**Directions**

- Place a large saucepot over medium heat. Add water, parsnips, potatoes, carrots, and onions. Do not cover; simmer for about 15 minutes until vegetables are soft.

- Remove from the heat source, drain, and sprinkle with olive and sugar. Return to the medium heat and cook until vegetables are somewhat golden.

- After that, transfer the vegetables to a serving plate. Enjoy.

**Nutritional facts per serving**

**Serving size**: ½ cup

Total carbohydrate 10 g, Cholesterol 0 mg, Calories 57, Monounsaturated fat 0.8 g, Trans fat 0 g Saturated fat Trace, Total fat 1 g, Dietary fiber 1 g, Sodium 24 mg, Added sugars 2 g, Protein 2 g.

# Sautéed Fresh Corn

Prosciutto is a spiced Italian beef that has fewer calories and less fat. You can substitute for smoked turkey if you do not have prosciutto.

**Yield:** 6 Servings

Healthy carb

Low Sodium

Low Fat

**Ingredients**

- 1 tsp of olive oil
- 2 cups of fresh corn kernels or frozen corn
- 2 oz of prosciutto, slice into skinny strips (approx. ½ cup)
- 1 tsp of crushed garlic
- 1 green bell pepper, seeded, cored and chopped

**Directions**

- Place a large frying pan over medium heat. Add the olive oil to pan and heat. Once hot, sauté the prosciutto for about 5 minutes until meat is crispy. Add the corn, garlic, pepper. While stirring infrequently, sauté for about 7 minutes until the kernels are soft.
- Remove from the heat source and serve hot.

**Nutritional facts per serving**

**Serving size:** About 3/4 cup

Calories 78, Cholesterol 8 mg, Total carbohydrate 11 g, Monounsaturated fat < 1 g, Trans fat Trace, Sodium 216 mg, Saturated fat 0.5 g, Total fat 2 g, Dietary fiber 1 g, Added sugars 0 g, Total sugars 4 g, Protein 4 g.

# Tangy Snap Bean

**Yield:** 10 Servings

Low Sodium

Healthy carb

Low Fat

**Ingredients**

- 1 ½ pound of fresh, canned or frozen snap bean
- ⅓ Cup of chopped sweet red bell peppers
- 4 ½ tsp of canola or olive oil
- 4 ½ tsp of water
- 1 ½ tsp of mustard
- 1 ½ tsp of vinegar
- ⅛ Tsp of garlic powder
- ¼ tsp of pepper
- ¼ tsp of salt

**Directions**

In a steamer basket over water, cook the beans and red peppers until crisp-tender and then set aside. In a medium bowl, combine all the remaining ingredients. Stir well to combine evenly. Move beans to a large serving dish, spoon the dressing over it and stir to be well coated. Serve immediately.

**Nutritional facts per serving**

**Serving size**: Approx ⅔ cup

Calories 42, Cholesterol 0 mg, Total carbohydrate 5 g, Monounsaturated fat 1.5 g, Trans fat 0 g, Saturated fat 0.3 g, Total fat 2 g, Dietary fiber 2 g, Added sugars 0 g, Sodium 72 mg, Protein 1 g.

# Creamed Swiss-chard

Yield: **8 Servings**

Healthy carb

**Ingredients**

- 2 tbsp of olive oil
- 3 garlic cloves, thinly sliced
- 1 ½ tbsp of unbleached all-purpose flour
- 1 ¼ cups of low-fat plain soy milk
- 1 tbsp of shredded Parmesan cheese
- ½ tsp of freshly ground black pepper
- 2 pounds of Swiss chard, rinsed, stemmed and slice diagonally into strips ½-inch wide

**Directions**

- Place a large skillet over medium heat. Pour the olive oil to the skillet to heat. Stir in the flour to form a smooth paste. While stirring, add the garlic and heat for about 30 seconds. Stir in soy milk and heat until the mixture is a bit thickens.
- After that, add the Swiss chard stir to be well coated. Cover the pot and heat about 2 minutes, until tender. Then add pepper and sprinkle with cheese. Serve immediately.

**Nutritional facts per serving**

**Serving size:** About 1 ½ cups

Total carbohydrate 8 g, Cholesterol < 1 mg, Calories 80, Monounsaturated fat 3 g, Trans fat 0 g, Saturated fat 1 g, Total fat 4 g, Added sugars 0 g, Total sugars 3 g, Dietary fiber 2 g, Sodium 265 mg, Protein 3 g.

# Yummy Mashed Cauliflower

**Yield:** 4 Servings

Healthy carb

Low Fat

Low Sodium

**Ingredients**

- 1 head cauliflower
- 1 white leek, cut into 4 pieces
- 1 tbsp of soft tub margarine, non-hydrogenated
- 1 clove garlic
- Pepper to taste

**Directions**

- Cut the cauliflower into bits. In a large pot, add cauliflower leeks and garlic in water and steam until soft, about 25 minutes.
- Add the vegetables in a blender or food processor and puree until smooth. Process a small amount at a time. If the vegetables seem dry, add a little amount of boiling water.
- Add margarine and pepper to taste, stir to combine well. Serve immediately.

**Nutritional facts per serving**

**Serving size:** 1 cup

Calories 67, Cholesterol 8 mg, Dietary fiber 2.5 g, Total carbohydrate 9 g, Monounsaturated fat 1 g, Trans fat 0 g, Saturated fat 1 g, Total fat 3 g, Sodium 60 mg, Added sugars 3 g, Protein 2 g.

# Minted Baby Carrots

**Yield: 6 Servings**

Healthy carb

Low Fat

Low Sodium

**Ingredients**

- 1 pound of baby carrots, washed (approx 5 ½ cups)
- 6 cups of water
- 1 tbsp of cornstarch
- ½ tbsp of minced fresh mint leaves
- ¼ cup of 100% apple juice
- ⅛Tsp of ground cinnamon

**Directions**

- Place a large pot over medium-high heat, pour the water, and add carrots. Cook for about 10 until tender-crisp. Drain water from carrots, place in a serving bowl, and set aside.
- Place a small saucepot over medium heat. Add the cornstarch and apple juice. Stir frequently about 5 minutes, until mixture thickens. Stir in the cinnamon and mint.
- Pour the apple juice mixture over the carrots and serve immediately.

**Nutritional facts per serving**

**Serving size**: Approx. ¾ cup

Calories 44, Cholesterol 0 mg, Total carbohydrate 10 g, Monounsaturated fat Trace, Trans fat 0 g, Saturated fat Trace, Total fat Trace, Dietary fiber 2.5 g, Added sugars 0 g, Total sugars 5 g, Sodium 51 mg, Protein 1 g.

# SOUP RECIPES

# Spicy Tomato Soup

**Yield:** 2 Servings

Low Fat

**Ingredients**

- 1 can of (10.5 oz) condensed low-fat, reduced-sodium tomato soup
- 1 can of (10.5 oz) fat-free milk
- 1 tbsp of sliced fresh cilantro or basil
- 1 medium tomato, diced
- 1 tbsp of freshly shredded Parmesan cheese
- 2 tbsp of croutons

**Directions**

Add the tomato soup and milk in a saucepot over medium heat. Stir to combine. Cook for about 10 minutes while stirring regularly. Then add the diced tomato and cilantro or basil. Cook for another 5 minutes, stirring infrequently.

To serve, spoon the soup evenly to individual serving dishes. Garnish with 1 tbsp of croutons and 1½ tsp of parmesan each. Serve hot.

**Nutritional facts per serving**

**Serving size**: Approx 1 ½ cups

Total carbohydrate 31 g, Cholesterol 5 mg, Calories 178, Sodium 220 mg, Monounsaturated fat 0.5 g, Trans fat 0 g, Saturated fat 1, Total fat 2 g, Added sugars 0 g, Total sugars 22 g, Dietary fiber 3 g, Protein 9 g.

# Savory Fennel and Potato Soup

**Yields:** 8 Servings

Healthy carb

High Fiber

Low Fat

Low Sodium

**Ingredients**

- 1 tsp of olive oil
- 2 large russet potatoes, peeled and chopped
- 1 large fennel bulb (approx. 2 pounds), finely sliced
- 2 tsp of fennel seeds, toasted
- 3 cups of low-sodium chicken stock
- 1 cup of sliced red onion
- 2 tsp of lemon juice
- 1 cup of fat-free milk

**Directions**

- Place a large saucepan over medium heat and add the olive. Once the oil is hot, add onion and fennel. Cook for about 5minutes until vegetables are tender. Add the potatoes, lemon juice, milk, and chicken stock and stir. Simmer covered about 15 minutes until potatoes are soft.

- In a food processor or blender, process the soup in batches (because it will be hot) until smooth.
- Transfer the soup back to the pan and place over heat to warm. Spoon the soup into individual serving dishes. Garnish with toasted fennel seeds. Enjoy

**Nutritional facts per serving**

Serving size: Approx ¾ cup

Calories 149, Cholesterol 0.5 g, Total carbohydrate 28 g, Monounsaturated fat 1 g, Trans fat 0 g, Saturated fat 0.5 g, Total fat 1.5 g, Dietary fiber 3 g, Added sugars 0 g, Total sugars 7 g, Sodium 104 mg, Protein 6 g.

## Creamy Wild Rice Soup

Dietitian's tip:

The blended white beans in this recipe provide creaminess, as well as protein and fiber.

**Yield:** 4 Servings

Healthy carb

High Fiber

**Ingredients**

- ½ tbsp of canola oil
- 1 cup chopped carrot
- ½ cup of cooked wild rice
- 1 cup prepared white beans, unsalted or ½ of a 15.5 oz can white beans

- 1 ½ cups of chopped yellow onion
- 2 cloves garlic, crushed
- 1 cup of chopped celery
- 1 tbsp of crushed parsley
- 1 ½ cups of finely sliced kale
- 1 tsp of fennel seeds, minced
- 2 cups reduced-sodium vegetable broth
- 1 tsp of freshly ground black pepper
- 2 cups of 1 percent milk

## Directions

- Rinse and drain the beans and then set aside.
- Add the canola oil to a saucepan and place over medium heat. Once the oil is hot, add onion, garlic, carrot, and celery and cook until a bit brown. Add parsley, kale, spices, and broth, stir and bring to a boil.
- Puree the beans with milk in a blender, and then pour beans mixture to the soup. Bring to a boil and add the wild rice. Allow it to cook for about 30 minutes. Remove from heat source. Serve immediately.

## Nutritional facts per serving

**Serving size**: Approx. 2 cups

Calories 236, Sodium 180 mg, Dietary fiber 7 g, Total carbohydrate 38 g, Monounsaturated fat 2 g, Trans fat 0 g,

Saturated fat 1 g, Total fat 4 g, Added sugars 0 g, Cholesterol 6 mg, Total sugars 12 g, Protein 12 g.

# Vichyssoise (Cold Potato and Leek Soup)

Wash and rinse leeks thoroughly before cooking as it tends to trap grit between the leaves.

**Yield:** 6 Serving

**Ingredients**

- 1 tbsp of olive oil
- 1 medium onion, thinly chopped
- 4 cups of chicken stock, unsalted
- 4 leeks (white bottoms with a touch of green), thinly chopped
- 4 medium potatoes, peeled and thinly chopped
- 6 tbsp of thinly chopped chives
- 2 cups of chilled evaporated skim milk
- ½ tsp of mace
- Freshly ground black pepper, to taste

**Directions**

- Add the olive oil to a large saucepot and place over medium heat. Once the oil is hot, add the onion and leek and sauté for 5 to 6 minutes, until tender. Add potatoes, mace and chicken stock. Sauté until potatoes are softened.
- Transfer the mixture into a food processor or blender. Puree until smooth. Afterward, transfer it back to a large bowl and place it inside the refrigerator.

- To serve, add the evaporated milk and stir well. Spoon into individual serving dishes and top each with one tbsp of chives. Then, and pepper to taste. Serve chilly

**Nutritional facts per serving**

**Serving size**: Approx. 1 cup

Dietary fiber 3 g, Calories 264, Trans fat 0 g, Saturated fat 1 g, Monounsaturated fat 2 g, Total fat 4 g, Total carbohydrate 44 g, Cholesterol 3 mg, Added sugars 0 g, Sodium 164 mg, Protein 13 g.

# Spiced Carrot Soup

**Yield:** 6 Servings

Low Fat

Healthy carb

**Ingredients**

- 10 medium to large carrots, scraped and diced
- 3 tbsp of all-purpose (plain) flour
- 1 ½ tbsp of sugar
- 2 cups of water
- ¼ tsp of ground nutmeg
- ¼ tsp of ground black pepper
- 2 tbsp of fresh parsley, sliced
- 4 cups of fat-free milk

**Directions**

Add the water, carrots, and sugar to a large saucepot and place over medium-high heat. Cover simmered about 20 minutes until carrots are soft. Remove from the heat source and drain the carrots. Set aside and reserve a little out of the liquid.

Combine the flour, nutmeg, pepper, and milk in another saucepot. While frequently stirring, cook until the mixture become thicken.

Combine the carrots and white sauce in a food processor or blender. Blend until smooth. If desired, add more liquid. Transfer into a serving dish and garnish with 1 tsp of parsley each. Serve hot.

**Nutritional facts per serving**

**Serving size**: Approx. 1½ cups

Dietary fiber 3 g, Cholesterol 3 mg, Total carbohydrate 27 g, Total carbohydrate 27 g, Trans fat 0 g, Saturated fat trace, Monounsaturated fat trace, Total fat trace, Calories 140, Added sugars 3 g, Sodium 164 mg, Protein 7 g.

# Creamy Asparagus Soup

This soup is a good source of iron, vitamins A and C, potassium selenium, magnesium, and folate. You can use broccoli instead of asparagus if you wish.

**Yield:** 6 Servings

Healthy carb

Low Sodium

**Ingredients**

- ½ pound of fresh asparagus or broccoli, slice into ¼-inch pieces
- 2 cups of chopped potatoes
- 2 stalks of celery, diced
- ½ cup of sliced onion
- 4 cups of water
- 2 tbsp of butter
- 1 ½ cups of fat-free milk
- ½ cup of whole-wheat flour
- Cracked black pepper, to taste
- Lemon zest, to taste

**Directions**

- Place a large saucepan over medium-high heat and add the water, asparagus, potatoes, celery, and onions. Allow it to boil. Once boiling, reduce the heat to low and simmer covered about 15 minutes, until vegetables are softened. Add butter and stir.

- Combine the milk and flour in a small bowl. Stir in the milk mixture into the saucepan. Stirring frequently, Increase the heat to medium and cook for about 7 minutes, until soup thickens. Remove from heat source and season with the black pepper and lemon zest to taste. Serve immediately.

**Nutritional facts per serving**

**Serving size**: Approx. 1 ½cups

Dietary fiber 3 g, Cholesterol 11 mg, Calories 140, Saturated fat 3 g, Monounsaturated fat 1 g, Trans fat Trace, Total fat 4 g, Total carbohydrate 22 g, Sodium 76 mg, Added sugars 0 g, Protein 6 g.

# French Savory Onion Soup

**Yield**: 8 Servings

Healthy carb

**Ingredients**

- 2 tsp of olive oil
- 6 cups of sliced onions
- 2 cups of water
- 6 cups of reduced-sodium beef stock
- 2 tbsp of reduced-sodium soy sauce
- 2 tbsp of fresh thyme
- 2 oz of grated gruyere cheese
- ¼ tsp of ground black pepper
- 2 bay leaves

**Directions**

- Place a large nonstick saucepan over medium heat and add the olive oil. Once the oil is hot, add onions and sauté for about 20 minutes, until golden browned, stirring frequently. Add the water, stock, soy sauce, thyme, pepper, and bay leaves. Simmer about 20 minutes. Once done, remove bay leaves.
- After that, heat oven to broil. Ladle soup into 8 individual serving dishes that are oven-proof and top with the grated cheese. Put serving the dishes on a

baking sheet and broil until cheese is melt, about 1 minute.

- To serve, top each serving dish with a few croutons or a small slice of toasted bread. Serve immediately.

**Nutritional facts per serving**

**Serving size:** 1 cup

Total carbohydrate 12 g, Cholesterol 9 mg, Calories 101, Monounsaturated fat 1 g, Trans fat 0 g, Saturated fat 2 g, Total fat 4 g, Dietary fiber 2 g, Total sugars 5 g, Sodium 317 mg, Protein 6 g.

# Mushroom Soup with Wild Rice

You can use any variety of mushrooms such as oyster, shitake, porcini, portabella or cremini for this soup. All of them have almost the same number of calories, and each has its unique flavor.

**Yield:** 4 Servings

Low Sodium

Healthy carb

**Ingredients**

- 1 tbsp of olive oil
- ¼ cup of sliced celery
- Half of a white onion, sliced
- ¼ cup of diced carrots
- 1 ½ cups of chopped fresh white mushrooms
- 2 ½ cups of fat-free, reduced-sodium chicken stock
- ½ cup of white wine
- 2 tbsp of flour
- 1 cup fat-free half-and-half
- ¼ tsp of dried thyme
- 1 cup of prepared wild rice
- Ground black pepper

## Directions

- Heat olive oil in a large saucepot over medium heat. Once the oil is hot, add onion, carrots, and celery and sauté until softened. Stir in the mushroom, chicken broth and white wine Cover and bring to a boil.

- Combine flour, half-and-half, pepper, and thyme in a medium bowl. Add the flour mixture to the hot pot and then stir in the wild rice. Let cook until thickened and bubbly, while stirring frequently. Serve immediately.

## Nutritional facts per serving

**Serving size**: Approx.1½ cups

Cholesterol 3 mg, Sodium 120 mg, Total carbohydrate 23 g, Calories 170, Trans fat 0 g, Monounsaturated fat 3 g, Saturated fat 1 g, Total fat 5 g, Added sugars 0 g, Dietary fiber 2 g, Protein 8 g.

# Steamed Salmon Potage

Salmon is an excellent source of heart-friendly omega-3 fatty acids.

**Yield:** 8 Servings

**Ingredients**

- 1 tsp of olive oil
- 1 clove of garlic, crushed
- ½ cup of sliced celery
- 2 ½ cups of frozen country-style hash browns with onion and green pepper
- 1 15 oz can low-sodium chicken stock
- 1 cup of frozen peas
- 1 cup of diced carrots
- ½ tsp of ground pepper
- 1 12 oz of can evaporated skim milk
- 6 oz of canned or pouched pink salmon (boneless)
- 1 can of (14 ¾ oz) unsalted cream-style corn
- ½ tsp of dill

**Directions**

- Heat olive oil in a large frying pan over medium heat. Add the celery and sauté about 10minutes. Then add garlic and cook for an additional 1 minute.

- Stir in the chicken stock, carrots, peas, hash browns, pepper, and dill and then bring to a boil. Once boiling, reduce the heat and simmer until the veggies are tender.

- After that, add the salmon and use a fork to split it into pieces. Add the corn and milk; simmer until cooked. Serve immediately.

**Nutritional facts per serving**

**Serving size**: Approx.1 cup

Total carbohydrate 26 g, Sodium 207 mg, Calories 166, Monounsaturated fat 1 g, Saturated fat 0.5 g, Total fat 2.5 g, Trans fat Trace, Added sugars 0 g, Dietary fiber 2 g, Cholesterol 18 mg, Protein 11 g.

# Petite Marmite Soup

**Yield:** 4 Servings

Healthy carb

High Fiber

Low Sodium

**Ingredients**

- 1 tbsp of olive oil
- 1 can of (16 oz or approx. 1 ½ cups) canned red kidney beans or chickpeas, rinsed and drained
- ⅓ Cup of sliced celery
- ½ cup of sliced onion
- 4 cups of fat-free chicken stock, unsalted
- 1 carrot, chopped
- 1 garlic clove, crushed
- 1 small zucchini, chopped
- 2 large tomatoes, seeded and diced
- ½ cup of sliced spinach
- ½ cup of uncooked whole-grain small shell pasta
- 2 tbsp of chopped fresh basil

**Directions**

- Heat olive oil in a large saucepot over medium heat. Once the oil is hot, add onion, carrots, and celery and cook for about 5 minutes, until the vegetables are tender.

- Stir in the garlic and let cook for one more minute. Add chicken stock, beans, tomatoes, pasta, and spinach and stir to combine. Allow to boil and simmer about 10 minutes. After that, add the zucchini and cook for an additional 5 minutes.

- Once done, remove from the heats source and add the basil.

- To serve, spoon soup in individual serving dishes

**Nutritional facts per serving**

**Serving size:** Approx.2 cups

Cholesterol 11 mg, Sodium 400 mg, Total carbohydrate 30 g, Trans fat 0 g, Saturated fat 1 g, Monounsaturated fat 3 g, Total fat 5 g, Dietary fiber 8 g, Calories 213, Added sugars 0 g, Protein 10 g.

## Conclusion

Pre-diabetes may progress into diabetes if a person doesn't pay attention to their diet and exercise management.

Nevertheless, through taking the right action, people with this ailment have a good chance to prevent a more severe condition that may occur in the future.

Printed in Great Britain
by Amazon